The Vegetable Spiralizer Cookbook

A BOUNTY OF PRAISE...

During the pre-launch stages of this publication, a few people received this book during a free giveaway promotion. Hear what some of these readers had to say about The Vegetable Spiralizer Cookbook:

"A great companion for my Paderno spiralizer! My husband and I are in our 60s and we have been looking for healthy vegetable noodle recipes. We have looked no further since we've gotten this book"
— **Gene Pearson, Boynton Beach, Florida**

"I got a free copy of this vegetable spiralizer cookbook during a free giveaway and I am absolutely pleased. Thanks to the author for filling a REAL need"
— **Tessa Levine, Portland, Oregano**

"I am feeling really excited about this collection of over 100 spiralizer recipes. I don't own a Paderno, but I am happy that these recipes work with my spiralizer as well. I have been on the Paleo Diet for about a year or so and I know that these recipes will be a worthy addition to my Paleo recipe collection"
— **Patsy Robinson, Cincinnati, Ohio**

"Excellent recipes for the spiralizer. I also love the fact that the recipes are all gluten-free"
— **Mia Thompson, West Des Moines, Iowa**

"A must for anyone who wants to stay healthy for life!"
— **Jessy Pearle, RD, New York**

"An outstanding resource for a healthy gluten-free diet"
—**Robert Vaughan, San Jose, California**

"This publication has changed the way I see veggies and the recipes are absolutely great"
—**Marcia Forbes, Scottsdale, Arizona**

"A wonderfully written and helpful book. Everyone can use this book and get good results. Thanks to the author for sharing her experience and recipes in this wonderful cookbook"
—**Jennifer Edwards, Oxford, Missouri**

"Truly a revelation. This book has completely changed my life. I will never be able to thank this author for giving away a valuable resource

that makes me feel like a new person"
— **Adam Coke, Plano, Texas**

"A great gift and practical guide for using spiralized vegetables to make healthy meals! I plan on buying several Paderno spiralizers as a holiday gift this year and I will definitely get copies of this cookbook to go along with each of them. I believe that if you've found this book, you've found a gem!"
— **Victoria Smith, Midvale, Utah**

The Vegetable Spiralizer Cookbook

101 GLUTEN-FREE, PALEO & LOW CARB RECIPES TO HELP YOU LOSE WEIGHT & GET HEALTHY USING VEGETABLE PASTA SPIRALIZER – FOR PADERNO, VEGGETTI & SPAGHETTI SHREDDERS

Works with Paderno, Veggetti and other Spaghetti Spiral Shredders, Makers or Slicers

Laura Moore

Chefon Press

DISCLAIMER

The publisher and author make no representations or warranties with respect to the accuracy or completeness of the contents of this work and specially disclaim all warranties, including warranties without limitation warranties of fitness for a particular purpose. No warranties may be created or extended by sales or promotions. The information and strategies herein may not be suitable for every situation. This material is sold with the understanding that the author or publisher is not engaged in rendering medical, legal, or other professional advice or services. If professional help is required, the services of a competent professional should be sought. Neither the publisher nor the author shall be liable for damages arising here from. The fact that an individual or organisation is referred to in this work as a citation and/or possible source of further information or resource does not mean the author or the publisher endorses the information of the individual or organisation that they/it may provide or recommend.

Many of the designations used by manufacturers and sellers to distinguish their products are claimed as trademarks. Any and all product names referenced within this book are the trademarks of their respective owners. None of these owners have sponsored, endorsed or approved this book. Always read all information provided by the manufacturer's product labels or manuals before using their products. The author and publisher are not responsible for product claims made by manufacturers.

Table of Contents

CHAPTER 14

CHAPTER 15

CHAPTER 16

CHAPTER 17

CHAPTER 18

CHAPTER 19

①

SPIRALIZING—THE HEALTHY EATING REVOLUTION!

Hi, I'm Laura and I love to spiralize! It was only two years ago since I ordered my first spiralizer and I still remember how excited I was. I felt as though I was just a little kid who was expecting a precious gift from Santa. I couldn't wait to have it in my kitchen. By the time my well anticipated spiralizer arrived, my kitchen was fully stocked with all sorts of vegetables. Aw well, time surely flies! Now, everyone in my home looks forward to my next interesting and tasty spiralized vegetable dish. Well, everyone except for my beloved cat, Molly. Instead, Molly usually spends her time licking away at the leftover sauce.

Admittedly, my spiralized cooking perfection didn't just happen overnight. At first, I wanted to turn just about any vegetable into noodles with my spiralizer. As time went by, I continued to experiment with different vegetables and recipes. It wasn't long before I was fully obsessed with using my veggie noodles to create interesting gluten-free meals. Overtime, I have solidified my experience and began to share my creative recipes with family and friends. But even more importantly, over a 2-year period, my spiralizer has dramatically changed my life. Apart from my family significantly improving our health, I have lost over 40 pounds. And for me, that's priceless. In this cookbook, I am excited and happy to share my experience and personal spiralized vegetable recipes with you and many others around the globe.

Like me, many food enthusiasts and busy cooks have become obsessed with turning vegetables into cute pasta noodles with their spiralizer. And by the way, it's absolutely exciting! Spiralizing your vegetables is simply a fun and healthy way to eat fewer calories, low carbs, eat gluten-free or just enjoy your vegetables.

There's no doubt that the spiralizer is an absolute genius and an essential part of a well-equipped kitchen. No surprises there. In fact, I believe that every new bride should be getting a vegetable spiralizer among her gifts. The spiralizer is just really great for everyone.

Interestingly, the vegetable spiralizer not only saves time, but it can be used to create fancy meals that can make an ordinary cook look like a pro. With a spiralizer, you can enjoy really hearty home-cooked meals without a lot of fuss. Better yet, the spiralizer can be used to create many healthy meals while also preserving the natural enzymes and valuable nutrients of raw vegetables and fruits. Several vegetables and fruits can be spiralized and can be prepared raw or cooked.

So, if you are living gluten-free and you've discovered the spiralizer, you should be celebrating! And if you love food and you want to lose weight, you can celebrate even more. In fact, with strong medical and scientific evidence concluding that there is a connection between diet and health, I believe that the vegetable spiralizer will play an important role in the next diet revolution. Welcome aboard—you're in for an exciting journey!

(2)

WHY YOU NEED THIS COOKBOOK

This cookbook is your ultimate resource for cooking healthy and delicious recipes with spiralized vegetables. The book is specially created with a unique collection of over 100 healthy and easy gluten-free spiralized recipes which are all themed in six (6) different categories. Furthermore, these recipes are all gluten-free, low in calories, low carb and are created to support a healthy lifestyle. Generally, you will find this book to be particularly helpful if you own a spiralizer or if you plan to get one. Even more specifically, you will find this book to be useful if you are looking for wholefood spiralized that are:

- Gluten-Free
- Weight Loss Friendly
- Paleo Friendly
- Dairy-Free
- Low Carb
- Low Calorie
- High Fiber

Considering all this, your gluten-free or weight loss journey will inevitably become more inspiring with these recipes. Furthermore, you don't have to be a rocket scientist to master the art of spiralized cooking with this cookbook. With the simple guidelines and procedures, you'll be successful in creating healthy and flavorful meals in a mere fraction of time. You'll start making tasty spiralized vegetable recipes that you and your family will love.

③

WHY SPIRALIZE?

There's more to spiralizing than the fun involved in making colorful and interesting shapes from your favorite spiralizable veggies and fruits. Without a doubt, spiralizing will change the way you usually eat and think about vegetables. Here are some reasons to start using your spiralizer as often as you can:

IT ENHANCES WEIGHT LOSS AND OVERALL GOOD HEALTH

Forget about fad diets! It is no longer a secret that by cutting carbs and calories you will automatically slash pounds or stones. Neither is it a secret that an increase in your fruit and vegetable intake will add more well needed fiber for a healthy diet. So, for those who want to seriously lose some weight, start spiralizing and change your life forever. Like me and many others, you'll find that spiralizing is a sure winner when it comes to optimum health. Here is a quick example of why this works. Compared to a regular serving of pasta, a serving of spiralized zucchini pasta contains 6-7 times less calories and carbs. This means that you could be cutting carbs and calories by up to a whopping 70 percent if you start making some of these healthy recipes with your spiralizer.

Ultimately, the more you cut carbs and calories, the more weight you'll lose. Also, by increasing the amount of fruits and

5

vegetables in your diet you will also be providing your body with essential nutrients for better health. So, if you simply switch from regular pasta to spiralized pasta, you'll be amazed at the results. Besides, with the added overall health benefits, you won't even miss having your regular pasta.

IT'S FAST AND EASY

As we all know it, the traditional way of preparing strips from vegetable may be quite tedious and time-consuming. On the contrary, with a vegetable spiralizer, preparing vegetable noodles is much easier and faster. After your vegetable has been secured or properly positioned in your spiralizer, the actual spiralizing process will take place in a mere minute or few. Now that your vegetable is spiralized it also cooks very quickly. For example, a batch of zucchini pasta normally cooks within 5 minutes and this happens to be less than half the time it would take to cook regular pasta. Additionally, cleaning up your spiralizer is very quick and also less messy when compared to the regular way of cleaning up after preparing vegetables with alternative tools.

IT IS A GREAT GLUTEN-FREE OR PALEO ALTERNATIVE!

Increased cases of gluten sensitivity or food allergies are common these days. With gluten being present in most processed and refined foods, more and more people are struggling to just simply maintain good health. Spiralizing your vegetables is absolutely a great solution for ditching refined foods and preparing fiber-rich and interesting gluten-free meals. Additionally, for the paleo dieters out there, spiralizing your vegetables will bring more excitement to your paleothic world. Essentially, the vegetable spiralizer helps to eliminate the craving for regular pasta.

IT ENCOURAGES CONSUMPTION OF RAW VEGETABLES

Most people are well aware that they need to increase their

daily intake of raw veggies and fruits. For decades, doctors have recommended that in order for our bodies to functionally get rid of toxins we should be eating five or more servings of raw veggies and fruits daily. But let's be honest, most of us are as busy as a bee and have very little time to spare for making raw veggie meals. With the spiralizer, you will be able to conveniently and easily prepare raw vegetables and fruits in a jiffy. Furthermore, by simply turning a handle (depending on which spiralizer you have), you could be making attractive and healthy raw vegetable spirals within a single minute. Based on the spiralizer's convenience and ease of use, you will eventually end up eating larger servings of vegetables and fruits. Moreover, as mentioned earlier, cleaning up with the spiralizer is less messy and much quicker than with the regular way of preparing vegetables.

YOUR KIDS WILL EAT MORE VEGETABLES

By turning your veggies into curly ribbon spirals and wiggly noodles your kids are more likely to become more interested in eating their veggies. For kids, the spiralizer brings much fun and excitement from the kitchen to the dining table. Besides, if you play all your cards right, their little tummies will be packed with those veggies before you know it. So, unlike the regular drills and hassle to get kids to eat the regular boring salads or steamed veggies, with the spiralizer your kids can enjoy encouraging vegetable snacks and other meals. Give your veggies a makeover—your kids will love it!

WORKING WITH THE BEST SPIRALIZERS

There are many spiralizers on the market, but all spiralizers are not created equal. Some spiralizers are battery operated while others are manually operated. I happen to own a manual one which is quite easy to use and does the spiralizing job quite well. Based on my experience and research, I will simply mention two top spiralizers which are the most popular and best products presently on the market. For sure, you may have your own favorites. Please be aware that I am not affiliated with any of these mentioned companies or brands. However, for the sake of some of my readers, I am making mention of these spiralizers in my cookbook.

The Paderno Spiralizer/Slicer

By now, you may be wondering which brand of spiralizer I have used to prepare my sumptuous spiralized vegetable dishes. Without further ado, it's the Paderno and I surely recommend it. The Paderno spiralizer can create really cute spirals of some of your favorite vegetables or even fruits. It comes with up to 3 or 4 sharp stainless steel blades (depending on the model) and a sturdy plastic BPA-free base frame that sits firmly on the kitchen counter. The Paderno manual provides an easy guide for assembling its parts and no tools are required for assembly. Once assembled, the Paderno spiralizer will do its job very quickly and works great for preparing larger servings of vegetable spirals.

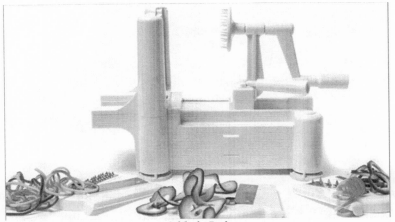

3-blade Paderno

With Paderno's 3 or 4 blade choices, you can create veggie spirals of spectacularly different shapes and sizes. So, whether you want curly ribbon-like spirals or thick or thin spaghetti-like strands, you can get the job done with the Paderno spiralizer. Here's a quick description of the blades and what they can do:

STRAIGHT BLADE (Spiral Shredder): This blade has a straight blade rather than a triangular-like blade and produces long ribbon-like pasta spirals. It is perfect for making spiralized cucumber and zucchini pasta ribbons as well as perfectly sized slices for potato or apple chips.

CHIPPER BLADE (Coarse Shredder): This blade has a large shredder blade and produces long and thicker spaghetti-like noodle spirals. It is perfect for making spiralized carrots, parsnips, zucchini and potatoes.

SHREDDER BLADE (Fine Shredder): This blade happens to be my favorite and has a fine shredder blade which produces thinner spaghetti-like spirals. It is perfect for spiralizing just about any vegetable or fruit.

ANGEL HAIR SHREDDER BLADE (only available with the 4-blade Paderno model): This is the newest blade option and it is the finest shredder blade of all the blades. It produces long and thin angel hair-like spaghetti spirals. It is also great for spiralizing any of your favorite spiralizable vegetables.

HOW TO SPIRALIZE: There is a neat and almost hidden storage compartment which is located under the base of the frame for blade storage. Simply push down a bit and pull forward in order to retrieve a blade of your choice. It is important that you ensure that the slicer's suction feet is firmly attached to the counter and that the blade is firmly secured (it usually clips when secured) in the slot before you attempt to spiralize your vegetable. After you have prepared your vegetable or fruit, simply place your vegetable in the center of the circular core of the blade and secure it firmly using the teeth (spike-looking) food holder on the opposite end. After the vegetable is securely held in place, push with the lower handle while also turning the side crank (handle with the food holder) in a circular clockwise motion. Turn your handle. Continue turning until you have enough spirals for your dish. Always remember to place a bowl to catch your spirals.

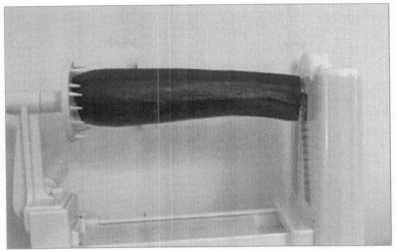

Zucchini setup for Paderno

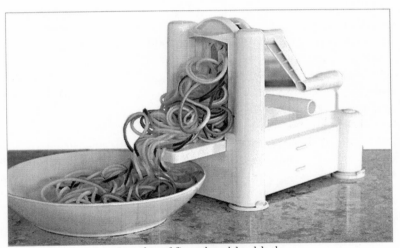

Results of fine shredder blade

CARE AND MAINTENANCE: The Paderno slicer isn't dishwasher safe, however, its detachable parts are quick and easy to clean. Sometimes it may seem difficult to clear the blades or the plastic food holder, but, there is no need to risk cutting your fingers. Simply get a new toothbrush (or small kitchen brush) in order to prevent cutting your hands or putting away a dirty spiralizer. To properly clean the spiralizer, use the

11

brush, along with running water and soap. Stainless steel chopsticks may also help to remove food particles that may remain in the core of the spiralizer. You may easily store the spiralizer in a cupboard or suitable kitchen compartment.

BEST VEGETABLES FOR PADERNO: This spiralizer can do all spiralizable vegetables and works great for squash, zucchini, potatoes, cucumbers, parsnips, rutabagas, apples and carrots. For the best results, choose vegetables and fruits that are about 5cm (2") in diameter or larger and no more than 25cm (10") in length and 18cm (7") in thickness whenever you go shopping. Also, the straighter the vegetable, the better the results.

The Veggetti Spiralizer

Many people have used the Veggetti spiralizer to get good results, even though it is of a completely different design from the Paderno. The Veggetti spiralizer is used like a pencil sharpener and has sharp stainless steel blades on each end or side. One end produces thin spirals while the other end produces thick spirals. The spiralizer also comes with a closed food holder cap on one end which can be used to easily hold and feed the vegetable into the spiralizer by a simple push and turn action. Additionally, the Veggetti spiralizer is easily grasped and works well for making smaller portions of veggie spirals. All parts of the Veggetti are pre-assembled and there is no assembling of parts required to set it up.

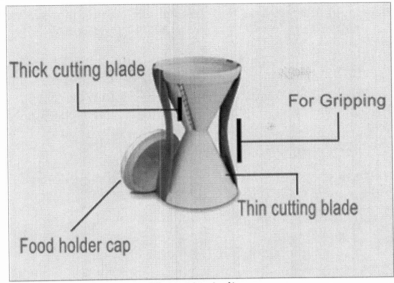

Veggetti spiralizer

HOW TO SPIRALIZE: Spiralizing vegetables in your Veggetti spiralizer is quite easy. You should start by washing your vegetable and trimming any unwanted part. You then firmly hold the middle of the metal handles and place the vegetable in either end of the spiralizer depending on whether you want thick or thin spirals. Hold the end of your vegetable and turn it in a pencil-sharpening motion until you have enough spirals for your dish. You may also use the food holder cap to hold the vegetable as it gets smaller or to prevent slippage. It is normal for vegetable drippings to be suctioned through the opposite bottom end of the Veggetti as you spiralize.

CARE AND MAINTENANCE: According to the manufacturers, the Veggetti is dishwasher safe. You should ensure that you wash the Veggetti spiralizer and its parts in luke warm soapy water or warm running water before each initial use. It doesn't usually come with a cleaning brush for washing, however, you could use your regular cleaning brush from your dishwasher or a new toothbrush to carefully clean the blades to remove food particles. You must be careful whenever you use the Veggetti as you wouldn't want to accidentally spiralize your fingers. For storing, it is small enough for storing in a suitable kitchen drawer.

BEST VEGETABLES FOR VEGGETTI: This spiralizer works best with cylindrical-shaped and cone-shaped vegetables that are between approximately 4cm (1½") and 7cm (2¼") in diameter. The Veggetti friendly vegetables includes: squash, zucchini, potatoes, cucumbers, carrots, parsnips and other similarly shaped veggies or fruits.

IMPORTANT: *These guidelines are not intended to be a substitute for the manufacturer's instruction manual*

(5)

SPIRALIZING POINTERS

B y using the spiralizer regularly, spiralized cooking will tend to become virtually foolproof and predictable. If you carefully follow the recipes in this book, you should be able to get perfect and delicious results every time. Here are a few pointers to help you stay on track:

- If your spiralizer didn't come with a separate cleaning brush, it is a great idea to purchase one. This will make it easier to remove vegetable particles that may be stuck in the blades or food holder (spikes) of your spiralizer.

- Serving and eating seemingly long vegetable spirals can be challenging. With this in mind, after you have spiralized your vegetable, it is a good idea to follow through with a kitchen scissors or shears and quickly clip your spirals to a regular pasta serving size.

- Water doesn't seep out of regular pasta or noodles, however, when it comes to vegetable spirals the opposite is true. Spiral seepage often results in a watery sauce while cooking or while the vegetable pasta sits in a sauce. You may avoid this by simply cooking and storing the veggie pasta and the sauce separately. After the veggie pasta is cooked, use a slotted spoon to remove them and use a paper towel to gently pat dry, then place the veggie spirals aside. You may then add your sauce to your spirals without worrying about a runny mess.

- Eating raw vegetable spirals is an easy way to get all the rich nutrients and live enzymes from your vegetables. Therefore, instead of cooking your raw spirals, you may also have them raw. Simply add your favorite sauce over your vegetables, allow it to sit for a minute and enjoy a healthy raw meal.
- Sometimes you may end up with scrap pieces of vegetables that don't have that noodle-like shape that you are looking for. You don't have to always throw away these pieces. You may consider using some of these pieces in salads or other dishes later on.
- A special note for cucumbers, in many instances, you may need to use paper towels to gently pat dry your spiralized cucumbers or other vegetables that have similar high water content. Doubling the paper towel sheets usually works well.

(6)

GLUTEN-FREE SPIRALIZING FOR BEGINNERS

If you're already familiar with living gluten-free and spiralizing you may skip this section and continue along. However, if you are a beginner, this section may be quite helpful.

SHOPPING

You should go shopping before you start your exciting gluten-free spiralizing journey. Planning is really worth every effort and will surely make things much easier. Besides, poor organization is the main reason for failures in general.

Before you go shopping, you should make a note of ingredients in the recipes that you will be preparing for about a week. Your shopping list should be mainly based on the ingredients in your chosen recipes. You should carefully create a shopping list before heading out to the food store. Apart from the specific ingredients of the recipes, your list should always include extra ingredients.

It is a great idea to clear your kitchen cabinets and refrigerator of the items that are not a part of the gluten-free

17

diet or items that will not positively contribute to your gluten-free lifestyle or goals. In doing so, you may need to get rid of unhealthy sugars, fats and carbs in order to avoid mistakenly adding them to a recipe or even feeling desirous of using them.

CHOOSING YOUR FOOD

- Whenever you go shopping you should ensure that you buy antibiotic-free and hormone-free meat, poultry and fish. You should look for free-range poultry and eggs as well as grass-fed beef, organic pork or wild fish. It is also important to choose freshly frozen meat for the benefit of healthy nutritional enzymes in your diet.
- When buying vegetables and fruits you should make every effort to buy fresh local vegetables and fruits that are certified to be organic. Even though organic food tends to be generally more expensive, sooner or later, the health benefits will far outweigh the cost. Compared to conventionally grown food, organic foods are healthier and contain lower levels of pesticides, hormones, and antibiotics than conventional.
- Whenever you go shopping, wherever possible, you should always choose the larger and straighter vegetable and fruits. Medium and large sizes are great for making large dishes, creating larger spirals and works well with most spiralizers.
- Whenever you go shopping and wherever possible, always choose tubular or cone-shaped vegetables. Vegetables with these shapes will feed easily into most spiralizers.
- Whenever you go shopping, always avoid vegetables with cracks as these tend to produce half-moon shaped spirals instead of long curly ones.

Essential Gluten-free Kitchen Tools

There are several essential tools that could make your gluten-free spiralizing lifestyle much easier. Though not all of these items are needed for the recipes in this book, they are simply essential items that you'll find useful in your kitchen.

Here is a quick list of some essential and common kitchen tools:

- ✓ A spiralizer
- ✓ A julienne/potato
- ✓ mandolin peeler
- ✓ A food processor
- ✓ Paper towels
- ✓ Stainless steel chopsticks
- ✓ Cleaning brush or toothbrush
- ✓ BPA-free plastic storage containers
- ✓ Pyrex glass storage containers (with lids)
- ✓ A ladle
- ✓ A colander
- ✓ Ziplock storage bags of different sizes
- ✓ A powerful blender
- ✓ A dutch oven
- ✓ A grill pan
- ✓ A set of good-quality knives
- ✓ Wooden cutting boards—use separate boards for animal products and fruits or vegetables
- ✓ An 8-inch nonstick sauté pan
- ✓ A 12-inch nonstick sauté pan (avoid non-stick pans with Teflon or other health risks due to poorer quality)
- ✓ An 8-quart stockpot
- ✓ Cooling rack
- ✓ 3 or 4 cookie or baking sheets
- ✓ Oven mittens
- ✓ Storage glass jars for condiments
- ✓ Natural parchment paper
- ✓ A lemon/citrus reamer
- ✓ A food mill/potato ricer
- ✓ A 2-quart saucepan with lid
- ✓ A 4-quart saucepan with lid
- ✓ A foil lined baking tray
- ✓ A coffee grinder for flaxseed or similar stuff
- ✓ Wire whisks
- ✓ Spring tongs
- ✓ Rubber spatulas
- ✓ Assorted measuring cups and spoons (1 quart, pint, 1 cup etc.) dry and liquid style
- ✓ A food scale
- ✓ Muffin pans
- ✓ Baking pans
- ✓ Skewers
- ✓ An instant-read chef's thermometer
- ✓ Timer
- ✓ Mixing bowls of different sizes
- ✓ Electric mixer

Please bear in mind that you may already have most of these items in your kitchen and that this is not a conclusive list.

SPIRALIZING WITHOUT A SPIRALIZER

The recipes in this cookbook will tend to work best with the Paderno Spiralizer, the Veggetti Slicer or other spiralizers with similar functionality. However, if your cute little kitchen tool hasn't yet arrived, do not despair. There's hope. You may use a julienne, potato or mandolin peeler to create noodle-like strips. These strips aren't really like those spirals created by a spiralizer; however, they may be used as substitutes to create healthy dishes as well.

USING A JULIENNE, POTATO OR MANDOLIN PEELER: These peelers will not spiralize vegetables like a spiralizer, however, they can be used to make thinner strands and may work particularly well with recipes that does not require cooking. By applying heat to thinner vegetable strands it may cause the strands to break and become mushy. For making spiral-like dishes, you will need to choose vegetable peelers that are made of stainless steel with sharp dual blades for peeling on one side and for making long, thin vegetable noodle-like strips on the other side. Note that the potato peeler may produce thicker and broader strands than a julienne peeler. Additionally, the vegetable peeler usually has an easy grasping handle and requires no assembly of parts. Not sure which peeler to buy?

You could try the *Zyliss Julienne Peeler* which is known to be quite efficient at producing thin and fancy vegetable strips.

HOW TO CREATE THE SPIRAL EFFECT: Creating thin vegetable noodle-like strips with your julienne, potato or mandolin peeler is easy. Simply prepare your vegetable, then keep peeling the vegetable right through until you have enough strips for your dish. You may end up with scrap pieces as you get closer to peeling the bottom of the vegetable. This is because the more you peel the vegetable, the thinner it will become and when it gets thinner it becomes more challenging to peel. You don't have to always throw away these vegetable scraps, you may also consider adding them to your salads, soups or stir-fry.

CARE AND MAINTENANCE: The julienne, potato or mandolin peeler is easily cleaned with a brush, a little soap and some running water. You should be careful whenever you use your vegetable peeler since the blades are very sharp. For storing, it is small enough for storing in a kitchen drawer.

BEST VEGETABLES: The vegetable peeler will not work for all vegetables. However, you may use it for spiralized squash, zucchini, potatoes, beets, cucumbers, squash and carrots dishes.

HOW ABOUT A KNIFE?

Well, I wouldn't recommend using a knife to create noodle-like strands for 3 main reasons. Firstly, by using a knife to create little noodle strips you'd better have some time on your hands. Using a knife tends to be quite a slow process and would be a poor choice for busy cooks who want to try their hand at spiralizing. Secondly, the knife is a terrible option if you want to create larger dishes. It would really be a challenging task to use a knife for creating a lot of noodle-like strips from your vegetable. Lastly, you have to be extremely careful with a knife as you aim to get smaller noodle-like strips. I wouldn't want you to accidently slip and cut your hands.

Nevertheless, in a worst case scenario, the knife may be used to create small noodle-like strips from your vegetables, but that's totally up to you.

Here's my disclaimer: *If you decide to use a knife for spiralizing your vegetables you are doing so at your own risk. The author of this publication does not endorse the use of knives for spiralizing vegetables.*

WHAT TO SPIRALIZE

As we know it, everyone has their favorite when it comes to vegetables. Besides, you may want to choose different vegetables based on your personal preferences or individual situations. So, just in case you want to explore your options and tweak a few recipes, here is a list of some vegetables that can be spiralized:

- ✓ Apples
- ✓ Beets
- ✓ Carrot
- ✓ Cucumber
- ✓ Eggplant
- ✓ Fennel
- ✓ Jicama
- ✓ Parsnip
- ✓ Plantain
- ✓ Radishes
- ✓ Rutabaga
- ✓ Squash (butternut squash or summer squash)
- ✓ Sweet potatoes
- ✓ Turnip
- ✓ Yam
- ✓ Zucchini (courgette/summer squash)

(8)

HOW TO SPIRALIZE

No matter what brand or style, generally all spiralizers work on the same principle. Of course, you may need to study your own spiralizer model and get fully acquainted with exactly how it works. Generally, you should be able to spiralize almost any spiralizable vegetable or fruit by following these simple 1-2-3 principles:

1. **Prepare the vegetable or fruit** by washing it first then opting to peel it based on personal taste or the recipe directions. Next, use a sharp knife to cut off the top and bottom ends. For most cylindrical or cone-shaped vegetables, you may need to evenly cut the vegetable in half. Note that preparation for some vegetables or fruits may differ based on the model of your spiralizer and your personal preference. With this in mind, reshaping your vegetable or fruit by making spiralizable slices or chopping the vegetable in half may be necessary based on your spiralizer model or your personal preference for the size and shape of your spirals. Note that most cylindrical shaped vegetables like the zucchini and cone-shaped vegetables like the parsnip or carrot works well for most spiralizers. Therefore, reshaping your vegetables in cylindrical or cone-like shapes is a great way to make them easily spiralizable.

2. **Secure or feed the vegetable onto your spiralizer for processing** according to the manufacturer's directions.

Your vegetable should be properly secured and aligned in your spiralizer.

3. **Spiralize your vegetable.** For manual spiralizers such as the Paderno, Veggetti and others, processing may involve manually turning a handle or the actual vegetable in order to produce veggie spirals. While for electronic or battery operated spiralizers, processing may involve simply loading or feeding the vegetable or fruit onto the spiralizer. Always pay attention while you spiralize in order to avoid accidents.

You may make reference to the section below in order to get a basic idea of how to spiralize most spiralizable vegetables. Please note that this is not a conclusive list, however, if you don't see the vegetable that you are looking for, there's a good chance that the spiralizing procedure for a vegetable of similar features is already included in the list. For example: Carrots and parsnips have similar features and would follow the same spiralizing procedure.

ZUCCHINI, SUMMER SQUASH, BUTTERNUT SQUASH

USING A PADERNO SPIRALIZER: You first wash your zucchini or squash then use a sharp knife to evenly chop off both ends. Peeling your zucchini is optional based on your taste, however, most people tend not to peel it. I usually peel my butternut or summer squash before spiralizing. Next, chop the zucchini or squash in half and choose your blade. The fine shredder blade for the spaghetti-like spirals works great here, however, you may also choose the blade according to your personal preference. Be reminded to place a bowl to collect your spirals. Next secure your zucchini or squash in the spiralizer and *SPIRALIZE*. You will notice that you end up with long and seemingly endless spaghetti-like strands. Simply use a clean kitchen scissors or shear to trim the noodles to a more manageable size. Your "zoodles" are now ready for preparation according to the recipe directions or for use as you desire.

USING A VEGGETTI SPIRALIZER: You first wash your zucchini or squash then use a sharp knife to evenly chop off the nose end (the side opposite to the stem). Peeling your zucchini is optional based on your taste; however, most people tend not to peel it. I usually peel my butternut or summer squash before spiralizing. Next, choose whether you will use the funnel end for thick or thin spirals. Hold the stem of the zucchini or squash then push and turn it in a pencil-sharpening motion until you have enough spirals for your dish. Remember to use the food holder cap as your vegetable gets shorter.

CARROT, PARSNIP

USING A PADERNO SPIRALIZER: You first wash your carrot or parsnip then use a sharp knife to evenly chop off both ends. Peel your carrot or parsnip with a vegetable peeler. Next, chop the carrot or parsnip in half and choose your blade. The fine shredder blade for the spaghetti-like spirals works great with carrots and parsnips. Be reminded to place a bowl to collect your spirals. Next secure your carrot or parsnip in the spiralizer and *SPIRALIZE.* Your carrot or parsnip noodles are now ready for preparation according to the recipe directions or for use as you desire.

USING A VEGGETTI SPIRALIZER: You first wash your carrot or parsnip then peel it with a vegetable peeler. Next, choose whether you will use the funnel end for thick or thin spirals. Insert the larger end of the vegetable into the center of the spiralizer. Hold the smaller end (cone-shaped tip) of the vegetable as a handle while pushing and turning it in a pencil-sharpening motion until you have enough spirals for your dish. Note that some people may insert the smaller end of the carrots first, even though this method also works, you may get better results by inserting the larger end first.

CUCUMBER

USING A PADERNO SPIRALIZER: You first wash your cucumber then use a sharp knife to evenly chop off both ends. Peeling your cucumber is optional based on your taste, however, most people tend not to peel it. Next, chop the cucumber in half and choose your blade. The straight blade for the ribbon-like spirals works best for cucumbers. Be reminded to place a bowl to collect your spirals. Next secure your cucumber in the spiralizer and *SPIRALIZE.* You will notice that a lot of liquid will seep out of your cucumber. In order to remove any excess seepage you will need to get four separated paper towels. Place two paper on a flat surface (a cutting board will work), then place the spiralized cucumbers on top of the paper towels. Place the other two paper towel on top of the cucumber spirals and apply gentle pressure which is enough to absorb the excess seepage. Your cucumber spirals are now ready for preparation according to the recipe directions or for use as you desire.

USING A VEGGETTI SPIRALIZER: You first wash your cucumber then use a sharp knife to evenly chop off the nose end (the side opposite to the stem). Peeling your cucumber is optional based on your taste, however, most people tend not to peel it. If you decide to peel it, use the food holder cap to avoid any slippage accidents. Next, choose whether you will use the funnel end for thick or thin spirals. Hold the stem of the cucumber then push and turn it in a pencil-sharpening motion until you have enough spirals for your dish.

SWEET POTATO/POTATO

USING A PADERNO SPIRALIZER: It is important that you choose tubular or cone-shaped sweet potatoes or potatoes for best results. You first wash your potato then use a sharp knife to evenly chop off both ends. Peel your potato with a vegetable peeler. Next, chop the potato in half and choose your blade. The fine shredder blade for the spaghetti-like spirals works great with potatoes as well. Be reminded to place a bowl to collect your spirals. Next secure your potato in the spiralizer and

SPIRALIZE. Your spiralized potato is now ready for preparation according to the recipe directions or for use as you desire.

USING A VEGGETTI SPIRALIZER: You first wash your potato then peel it with a vegetable peeler. Resize or reshape as needed if the potato is too large for the Veggetti. Next, choose whether you will use the funnel end for thick or thin spirals. Insert the potato into the center of the spiralizer. Use the Veggetti food holder cap to secure the potato then while pushing, turn it in a pencil-sharpening motion until you have enough spirals for your dish.

BEET, TURNIP, RADISH, JICAMA, RUTABAGA (SWEDES)

USING A PADERNO SPIRALIZER: You first wash your vegetable then use a sharp knife to evenly chop off both ends. If you are spiralizing beets, use a food gloves to avoid messy hands and kitchen. Peel your vegetable with a vegetable peeler. Next, choose your blade. The fine shredder blade for the spaghetti-like spirals works great with these vegetables as well. Be reminded to place a bowl to collect your spirals. Next secure your vegetable in the spiralizer and *SPIRALIZE.* Your veggie noodles are now ready for preparation according to the recipe directions or for use as you desire.

USING A VEGGETTI SPIRALIZER: You first wash your vegetable then peel it with a vegetable peeler. Remember to wear a food gloves if you are spiralizing beets. Resize or reshape your vegetable to fit the Veggetti if it is too large. Next, choose whether you will use the funnel end for thick or thin spirals. Insert the vegetable into the center of the spiralizer and while pushing, turn it in a pencil-sharpening motion until you have enough spirals for your dish. If your spirals don't turn out to be perfect, the reason for this may be that the Veggetti doesn't always do best with vegetables that are not cylindrical or cone-like in shape.

CABBAGE

USING A PADERNO SPIRALIZER: You first wash your vegetable then use a sharp knife to chop off the bottom end. Peel the outer cabbage layer with your hand. Next, choose your blade. The coarse shredder blade or the straight blade works great with cabbage. Be reminded to place a bowl to collect your spirals. Next secure your vegetable in the spiralizer and *SPIRALIZE.* Stop and go again if necessary. Your spiralized cabbage is now ready for preparation according to the recipe directions or for use as you desire.

Unfortunately, based on the shape of the cabbage, it doesn't work well in the Veggetti or other similarly shaped vegetable slicers. If you don't have a Paderno spiralizer, you may make regular shredded cabbage with a cabbage shredder.

IMPORTANT: *These guidelines are not intended to be a substitute for the manufacturer's instruction manual*

9

STORAGE TIPS

W ant to speed up your spiralized cooking for a few days or maybe a week? For some reason or another you may want to store some spiralized vegetables. Maybe you have spiralized too much for your dish or maybe you simply want to plan ahead. Storing your vegetables in order to preserve the safety and quality is essential when it comes to storage. Food safety is important for avoiding food contamination while food quality is important for preserving the consumable freshness of your vegetables. Even though not all spiralized vegetables have the same levels of perishability, most may last between 2-4 days on average in the refrigerator or freezer. Storage methods may vary for different vegetables when it comes to the preservation of freshness and overall quality. The reason for this is that some vegetables are naturally more suited for storage than others. Based on this fact, you should read the *Food Quality Storage Considerations* below for a few tips on storing commonly spiralized vegetables.

FOOD SAFETY STORAGE CONSIDERATIONS

- Do not buy bruised vegetables and fruits since they usually tend to spoil very quickly.
- Always prepare your vegetables and fruits with clean hands and kitchen utensils that have been washed with soap and water.

- Wash all vegetables and fruits with running water before use even if you plan to peel it before spiralizing. You may even use a brush to wash firm vegetables.
- Simply use a paper towel to dry your pre-washed vegetables and fruits to further lessen the presence of any surface bacteria.
- Ensure that your refrigerator is clean and has a temperature of 40 degrees Fahrenheit or lower.
- Use clean BPA-free and freezer-safe plastic storage containers or pyrex glass storage containers with lids to store your spiralized vegetables. A BPA-free re-sealable bag may also be used as a storage container.
- Aim to use separate cutting board and other utensils for your vegetables and avoid using the same utensils for meats and vegetables.
- Do not use or spiralize a vegetable or fruit that has already started to decay.

FOOD QUALITY STORAGE CONSIDERATIONS

Spiralized Zucchini – Zucchini pasta should not be stored in the freezer or else it will become quite soft and slushy and lose its freshness. For maintaining freshness, the refrigerator is best for storing your spiralized zucchini and it may last for about 4 days and if you are lucky it might last for 5 days. Usually, water tends to seep from the zucchini over time; however, you may gently pat dry any excess moisture with 2 sheets of paper towels both before and after refrigeration. Before placing your spiralized zucchini in a storage container, you may also consider adding 2 sheets of paper towels at the bottom of the container.

Spiralized Cucumbers – As with zucchini, cucumber pasta should not be stored in the freezer or else it will become quite soft and soggy and lose its freshness. For maintaining freshness, the refrigerator is best for storing your spiralized cucumber and it may last for about 2-4 days. Usually, water tends to seep from the cucumber over time; however, you may gently pat dry any excess moisture with 2 sheets of paper towels both before and after refrigeration. Before placing your spiralized cucumber in a storage container, you may also consider adding 2 sheets of paper towels at the bottom of the container.

Spiralized Carrots – Spiralized carrots usually store well in the refrigerator, however, you should expect a little dryness since they tend to dehydrate quite easily. Carrots tend to last for about 5 days in the refrigerator.

Spiralized Butternut Squash – Even though it will wither a bit, butternut squash is best if stored in the freezer and usually cooks easily after it is thawed. It may last for about 5 days in the freezer.

Spiralized Potatoes – Potatoes should not be stored in the refrigerator or else it will become quite soft and breakable and lose its freshness. For maintaining freshness, the freezer is best for storing your spiralized potatoes and it may last for about 4 days. You may gently pat dry any excess moisture with 2 sheets of paper towels after it is thawed.

10

GLUTEN-FREE BASICS

People go gluten-free for lots of reasons, however, most people adapt to a gluten-free diet due to gluten allergies. On a gluten-free diet, wheat, grains and their by-products are entire excluded. Hence, with the exclusion of wheat and grains from a gluten-free diet, it is not uncommon for gluten-free converts to experience challenges in maintaining a healthy fiber-rich diet. With this in mind, the spiralizer turns out to be a perfect solution to the gluten-free dieter's desire for healthy meals that are also rich in fiber.

Basically, the term gluten is commonly used to refer to a complex protein that is in grains such as wheat, oat, barley and rye. Scientific and medical studies have come to agree that it is very difficult for the stomach to digest the complex gluten protein. Whenever the stomach is forced to digest these hard to digest proteins, it will often remain undigested in the body and causes far-reaching health problems in the process or over time. Some of the health problems that may be triggered from gluten consumption includes: Celiac Disease, Collitis, Chron's Disease, Irritable Bowel Syndrome, Neurological Disorders, Obesity and other chronic diseases.

Today, gluten is present in most processed foods. As such, the manufacturers of processed wheat and grains have been intricately involved in the gluten distress of our population. Through the mass production and distribution of gluten products, the consumption of gluten has understandably

32

become increasingly popular over the last decades. Consequently, most processed foods and even medications have been found to contain gluten.

GLUTEN-FREE HEALTH BENEFITS

The health benefits of living on a gluten-free diet are increasingly becoming widely acknowledged by scientists and doctors alike. Grounded on considerable scientific and medical evidence, living without gluten has many possible benefits and may lead to:

- ✓ Significant weight loss
- ✓ Improvement in gastrointestinal health issues
- ✓ Increased vitality
- ✓ Reduced bloating and gas
- ✓ Decreased risk of heart disease
- ✓ Improvement in allergy control
- ✓ Strengthening of the immune system
- ✓ Improvement in brain health
- ✓ Decreased cancer risk
- ✓ Decreased risk of celiac disease
- ✓ Improvement and decreased risk in diabetes
- ✓ Improvement in overall healthy

All in all, gluten has been found to negatively affect the health of many people. Consequently, even if you've not identified any gluten sensitivities, you could tremendously improve your health by avoiding gluten entirely. Additionally, by incorporating the use of the spiralizer into a gluten-free diet, excitement lies ahead. Lose weight, live longer and feel better—go gluten-free with your spiralizer!

⑪

HOW TO USE THIS COOKBOOK

As mentioned earlier, you should familiarize yourself with exactly how your spiralizer model works. Hence, before you begin spiralizing, you should take some time to read your spiralizer instruction book and to practice assembling your spiralizer properly if necessary. By doing this, you'll be able to approach each recipe with confidence and achieve perfect results every time. Also, you'll learn how to properly and safely care for your spiralizer.

After choosing a recipe in this book, you should follow the specific recipe directions. Whenever a recipe lists a specific spiralized vegetable as an ingredient, you should use your spiralizer model according to the manufacturer's instructions. If necessary, you may also refer to the *"How to Spiralize"* guidelines in this book. However, please note that these guidelines are not intended to be used as a substitute for the manufacturer's instructions. By referring to the *"How to Spiralize"* guidelines, you should get a good idea of how simple it can be to start spiralizing. If you are a beginner to spiralizing, don't focus too much on the possible little glitches such as broken spirals or struggling with the very hard vegetables. Instead, place most of your focus on getting the right nutrients and enjoying your meal. With time, you'll be rolling out those perfect spirals before you know it.

Moreover, for ease of use and wholesome variety, this cookbook is nicely themed into six (6) different recipe categories:

- **EGG RECIPES** – these recipes consist of a variety of spiralized vegetable noodles with an interesting egg combination and other healthy ingredients. Some of these recipes are perfect for a nice and healthy breakfast.
- **MEATLESS RECIPES** – these recipes consist of a variety of spiralized vegetable noodles combined with a variety of sauces. Most of these recipes will not require cooking and are packed with nutritious enzymes. This section is the perfect pick for those "no-cooking" moments and could be a haven for raw food enthusiasts.
- **BEEF, PORK & LAMB RECIPES** – these recipes consist of a variety of spiralized vegetable noodles combined with interesting beef, pork and lamb dishes. This section is perfect for creating intriguing dinner and lunch menus.
- **FISH & SEAFOOD RECIPES** – these recipes consist of a variety of spiralized vegetable noodles combined with a variety of fish and seafood dishes. This section is also perfect for creating intriguing dinner and lunch menus. A great pick for all seafood lovers!
- **POULTRY RECIPES** – these recipes consist of a variety of spiralized vegetable noodles combined with a variety of chicken and turkey dishes. This section is also perfect for creating intriguing dinner and lunch menus. Interesting soups, salads and more are included in the poultry section.
- **HOLIDAY RECIPES** – these recipes consist of a variety of spiralized vegetable noodles combined with a variety of dishes that are perfect for holidays or special occasions. This section is perfect for creating intriguing and even elegant dinner and lunch menus. You may find a few desserts here as well.

IMPORTANT: *Most of the recipes in this cookbook work well with the Paderno's Fine Shredder Blade for creating spaghetti-like spirals. However, please feel free to choose blades according to your personal taste, preference and spiralizer model. Let your spiralizing journey be a flexible and fun-fulfilled one!*

12

LET'S START SPIRALIZING!

The Vegetable Spiralizer Cookbook consists of over 100 healthy and mouthwatering spiralized vegetable recipes. These recipes are specially created to help you restore your overall health and lose weight. Furthermore, this cookbook will help you to cook a perfectly tasty meal every time.

Whichever recipe you choose from this special collection of recipes, it's entirely up to you. Simply follow the recipe directions, then preparing and cooking spiralized vegetable meals will become surprisingly easy. Please feel free to make your own ingredient substitutions to suit your tastes or individual situations.

I have spent a lot of time to bring these recipes to perfection, but sometimes it's impossible to catch it all. So, if you see any obvious errors made in this book, please send me an email at: laura@weightlosspeeps.com. I will be very grateful for your feedback.

Now, it's time to start using your spiralizer to create healthy, easy and heart-warming gluten-free meals.

Let's start spiralizing those veggies!

EGG RECIPES

Spiralized Beet Omelet

This recipe will make one of the most delicious omelets with spiralized beet, scallions and avocado. This omelet is great for weekday mornings.

MAKES: 2 servings
PREPARATION TIME: 15 minutes
COOKING TIME: 11 minutes

Ingredients

2 tablespoons Extra Virgin Olive Oil
2 small Beets, peeled and spiralized
4 large Organic Eggs
Sea Salt, to taste
Freshly Ground Black Pepper, to taste
1 small Avocado, peeled, pitted and cubed
1 Scallion, chopped

Directions

1. In a large skillet, heat 1 tablespoon of the oil on a medium heat. Add the spiralized beet to the skillet and cook for 6 to 7 minutes before removing from the heat and setting aside.
2. Meanwhile, in a bowl, add the eggs and seasoning, and beat well. In a large frying pan heat the remaining oil on a medium heat. Add the beaten eggs and, with a wooden spoon, spread the eggs towards the edges of the pan. Cook for 1 to 2 minutes. Place the beets and avocado over the eggs. Carefully fold the omelet in half. Cook for a further 2 minutes.
3. Top with the scallions and serve hot.

Zucchini Kale Frittata

This frittata is packed with healthy vegetables like spiralized zucchini and kale, and proteins of eggs. The zucchini noodles add a great crunch in this frittata.

MAKES: 4 servings
PREPARATION TIME: 15 minutes
COOKING TIME: 25 minutes

Ingredients

1 tablespoon Extra Virgin Olive Oil
1 Garlic Clove, minced
3 Cups Fresh Kale, trimmed and chopped
1 large Zucchini, spiralized
Sea Salt, to taste
Freshly Ground Black Pepper, to taste
12 Organic Egg Whites, beaten

Directions

1. Preheat the oven to 375 degrees F.
2. In an oven proof skillet, heat the oil on a medium heat. Sauté the garlic for about 1 minute. Add the kale and cook for 3 to 4 minutes, or until the kale is just wilted. Transfer half of the kale onto a plate. Place the spiralized zucchini over the kale. Place the remaining kale over the zucchini and sprinkle with salt and black pepper. Spread beaten egg whites over the kale and cook for a further 2 minutes.
3. Transfer the skillet into oven and bake for 15 to 18 minutes.

Sweet Potato Breakfast Bake

This is an awesome and delicious recipe for breakfast or brunch.
This is a dish that the whole family will enjoy.

MAKES: 4 servings
PREPARATION TIME: 15 minutes
COOKING TIME: 35 minutes

Ingredients

2 tablespoons Extra Virgin Olive Oil
1 large Sweet Potato, peeled and spiralized
1 White Onion, chopped
2-3 Garlic Cloves, minced
Sea Salt, to taste
Freshly Ground Black Pepper, to taste
10-12 Organic Eggs

Directions

1. Preheat the oven to 350 degrees F.
2. In an oven proof skillet, heat the oil on a medium heat. Add the spiralized sweet potato and onion and cook for 8 to 9 minutes. Add the garlic and cook for 1 minute more. Carefully, crack the eggs over the sweet potato mixture.
3. Transfer the skillet into oven and bake for 20 to 25 minutes.

Carrot Medley Egg Salad

This is a tasty and fun pasta salad for the summer that has a crunchy texture. This salad is a perfect dish to bring to potlucks.

MAKES: 2 servings
PREPARATION TIME: 20 minutes

Ingredients

1 small Head of Broccoli, with stem
2 medium Carrots, peeled and spiralized
¼ cup Red Onion, chopped
3 Organic Hard Boiled Eggs, chopped
¼ cup Fresh Basil, chopped
1 Garlic Clove, minced
½ teaspoon Lime Zest, freshly grated
2 tablespoons Extra Virgin Olive Oil
1 tablespoon Fresh Lime juice
Water, as required
Sea Salt, to taste
Freshly Ground Black Pepper, to taste
2 tablespoons Pumpkin Seeds, roasted

Directions

1. Cut the broccoli florets into bite size pieces and spiralize the stem. Transfer the chopped broccoli florets and spiralized stem into a large serving bowl.
2. Add the carrot, onion and egg into the bowl with the broccoli and mix. In a food processor, add the remaining ingredients, except for the pumpkin seeds, and pulse until pureed. Pour the mixture over the vegetables and toss to coat.

3. Garnish with the pumpkin seeds and serve.

Sweet Potato Fry-up

This is a healthy yet delicious breakfast recipe for the whole family. This dish combines the delicious flavors of sweet potato and bell peppers with eggs and seasoning.

MAKES: 2 servings
PREPARATION TIME: 15 minutes
COOKING TIME: 18 minutes

Ingredients

3 tablespoons Extra Virgin Olive Oil
2 Garlic Cloves, minced
1 large Sweet Potato, peeled and spiralized
1 small White Onion, chopped
1 Red Bell Pepper, seeded and chopped
1 Green Bell Pepper, seeded and chopped
½ teaspoon Dried Thyme, crushed
¼ teaspoon Cayenne Pepper
Sea Salt, to taste
Freshly Ground Black Pepper, to taste
½ cup Cooked Chicken, shredded
4 Organic Eggs
1 tablespoon Fresh Basil, chopped

Directions

1. In a large skillet, heat 1 tablespoon of oil on a medium heat. Sauté 1 minced garlic clove for 1 minute. Add the spiralized sweet potato and cook for 6 to 8 minutes. Transfer onto a plate.
2. Meanwhile, in another skillet, heat 1 tablespoon of oil on a medium heat. Add the remaining garlic and sauté for 1

minute. Add the onion, bell peppers, thyme and seasoning and cook for 4 o 5 minutes. Stir in the chicken. Transfer the chicken mixture over the sweet potato.

3. In a frying pan, heat the remaining oil on a low heat. Carefully, crack the eggs into the frying pan. Spoon the hot oil over the whites until they are set, and spoon the oil over the yolks only a couple of times as the yolks should be runny. Cook for about 3 to 4 minutes. Top the chicken and sweet potato with the fried eggs. Garnish with fresh basil and serve.

Chiso Egg Rolls

This is a simple and easy recipe for breakfast. The sweetness of the sweet potato combined with the saltiness of grilled chicken make for a great pairing with the creamy avocado.

MAKES: 2 servings
PREPARATION TIME: 15 minutes
COOKING TIME: 11 minutes

Ingredients

*2 large Lettuce Leaves, pat dried
1 medium peeled, pitted and mashed Ripe Avocado
1½ tablespoons Extra Virgin Olive Oil
1 large Sweet Potato, peeled and spiralized
4 Organic Eggs, beaten
Sea Salt, to taste
Freshly Ground Black Pepper, to taste
¼ cup Grilled Chicken, shredded*

Directions

1. Arrange both lettuce leaves in 2 serving plates.
2. In a large skillet, heat 1 tablespoon of the oil on a medium heat. Add the spiralized sweet potato and cook for 6 to 8 minutes. Transfer the sweet potato noodles onto a plate. In the same skillet, heat the remaining oil on a medium heat. Add the eggs and sprinkle with salt and black pepper. Cook the eggs until they are done, for 2 to 3 minutes, before removing them from the heat.
3. Evenly place the mashed avocado over both lettuce leaves. Place the sweet potato over the avocado. Arrange the scrambled eggs over the sweet potato noodles, and

top with the shredded chicken. Carefully roll the lettuce leaves and serve.

Tropical Egg Mix

This salad has a wonderful flavor and texture. The use of celery adds a refreshingly tangy touch to this dish.

MAKES: 2 servings
PREPARATION TIME: 15 minutes

Ingredients

1 medium Zucchini, spiralized
1 medium Cucumber, spiralized
½ cup Grilled Salmon, cut into bite size pieces
½ cup Celery, chopped
½ cup Organic Coconut Milk
1 small Garlic Clove, minced
Sea Salt, to taste
Freshly Ground Black Pepper, to taste
2 large Organic Hard Boiled Eggs

Directions

1. In a large serving bowl, mix together the zucchini, cucumber, salmon and celery. In another bowl, combine together the coconut milk, garlic and seasoning. Pour the mixture over the vegetables and toss to coat.
2. Chop the eggs and place them on top of the dish before serving.

Yellow Spinach Frittata

This is a wonderfully delicious frittata for a fabulous weekend.
This delicious dish can be eaten at any time of the day.

MAKES: 2 servings
PREPARATION TIME: 15 minutes
COOKING TIME: 25 minutes

Ingredients

½ cup Organic Egg Whites
4 Organic Eggs
1 large Yellow Squash, spiralized and sliced into 3-inch
pieces
1 tablespoon Extra Virgin Olive Oil
2 Garlic Cloves, minced
2 cups Fresh Spinach, chopped
1 cup Red Bell Pepper, seeded and chopped
Sea Salt, to taste
Freshly Ground Black Pepper, to taste

Directions

1. Preheat the oven to 350 degrees F. In a large bowl, beat together the egg whites, eggs and seasoning. Stir in the spiralized squash and set aside.
2. In a large oven proof skillet, heat the oil on a medium heat. Sauté the garlic for about 1 minute. Add the spinach and bell peppers and cook for 3 to 4 minutes. Stir in the egg mixture.
3. Transfer the skillet into the oven and bake for about 20 minutes.

Broccoli Egg Combo

This is one of best dishes for a weeknight dinner. The combination of fried eggs, shrimp and broccoli with spiralized zucchini creates a warm texture.

MAKES: 2 servings
PREPARATION TIME: 20 minutes
COOKING TIME: 15 minutes

Ingredients

2 tablespoons Extra Virgin Olive Oil
2 large Organic Eggs
1 cup Broccoli Florets
1 small Onion, chopped
1 medium Red Bell Pepper, seeded and chopped
1 teaspoon Garlic, minced
1 teaspoon Fresh Ginger, minced
Sea Salt, to taste
Freshly Ground Black Pepper, to taste
1 teaspoon Coconut Vinegar
3 tablespoons Coconut Aminos
1 teaspoon Organic Honey
6-8 Jumbo Shrimp, peeled and deveined
2 medium Zucchinis, spiralized
½ teaspoon toasted Black Sesame Seeds

Directions

1. In a small skillet, heat 1 teaspoon of oil. Add the eggs and cook, whilst stirring, for 2 to 3 minutes. Remove the eggs from the pan and set to one side.
2. In a large skillet, heat the remaining oil on a medium

heat. Add the broccoli and cook for 3 to 4 minutes. Add the onion, bell pepper, garlic and ginger and cook for 2 to 3 minutes. Season with salt and black pepper. Add the shrimp and cook for about 2 minutes.

3. Meanwhile, in a bowl mix together the vinegar, coconut aminos and honey. Add in the scrambled eggs, spiralized zucchini and honey mixture and cook for 2 to 3 minutes. Top with the sesame seeds and serve.

Sweet Potato Prix

This is a savory and delicious way to enjoy the combination of sweet potato and eggs for breakfast. These baked sweet potato noodles are really delicious.

MAKES: 4 servings
PREPARATION TIME: 15 minutes
COOKING TIME: 30 minutes

Ingredients

2 medium Sweet Potatoes, peeled and spiralized
4 tablespoons Extra Virgin Olive Oil
1 teaspoon Chili Powder
Sea Salt, to taste
Freshly Ground Black Pepper, to taste
4 large Organic Eggs

Directions

1. Preheat the oven to 450 degrees F and line a baking sheet with parchment paper.
2. Place the spiralized sweet potato onto the prepared baking sheet. Drizzle the potato with 2 tablespoons of oil and sprinkle with the seasoning. Bake for about 30 minutes, tossing once after 15 minutes.
3. Meanwhile, in large pan, boil water on a medium-high heat. Reduce the heat to medium. Crack 1 egg into a bowl. Carefully pour the egg into the pan of boiling water. Repeat with the remaining eggs. Cook for 2 to 3 minutes, or until cooked. Place the poached eggs over the sweet potato noodles and serve.

Almond Zucchini Scramble

This recipe will create a large bowl of warm and scrumptious zucchini and eggs. Enjoy this dish which is packed with healthy proteins.

MAKES: 2 servings
PREPARATION TIME: 15 minutes
(plus time to marinate)
COOKING TIME: 10 minutes

Ingredients

2 medium Zucchinis, spiralized
Sea Salt, to taste
1 tablespoon Extra Virgin Olive Oil
½ teaspoon Extra Virgin Olive Oil
1 tablespoon Almond Flour
1 Garlic Clove, minced
3 Organic Eggs
Freshly Ground Black Pepper, to taste
¼ cup freshly chopped Cilantro Leaves

Directions

1. Place the spiralized zucchini into a colander and sprinkle with salt. Set aside for at least 20 minutes. Drain well and pat dry with a paper towel. Meanwhile, in a nonstick skillet over a medium heat, mix together ½ teaspoon of oil, almond flour and a pinch of salt. Cook, stirring continuously, for 1 minute before removing from the heat and setting aside.
2. In another skillet, heat the remaining oil on a medium heat. Add the spiralized zucchini and cook for 1 to 2

53

minutes. Transfer the zucchini into a bowl. In the same skillet, add the garlic and sauté for about 1 minute. Add the eggs and cook, stirring, for 2 to 3 minutes. Stir in the noodles and cilantro and cook for 2 minutes more.

3. Top with toasted almond flour and serve.

Jicama Deluxe

This is an amazing and tasty way to incorporate jicama into your daily life. Baked jicama with eggs makes a healthy meal for all.

MAKES: 4 servings
PREPARATION TIME: 15 minutes
COOKING TIME: 34 minutes

Ingredients

1 large Jicama, spiralized
5 tablespoons Extra Virgin Olive Oil
1 teaspoon Cayenne Pepper
Sea Salt, to taste
Freshly Ground Black Pepper, to taste
8 large Organic Eggs

Directions

1. Preheat the oven to 400 degrees F and lightly grease 2 baking sheets.
2. Arrange the spiralized jicama on the prepared baking sheets. Drizzle with 2 tablespoons of oil and sprinkle with spices. Bake for about 30 minutes, flipping once after 15 minutes.
3. Meanwhile, in a large frying pan heat the remaining oil on a low heat. Carefully, crack the eggs into the pan. Spoon the hot oil over whites until set and spoon the oil over yolks only a couple of times as the yolks should be runny. Cook for 3 to 4 minutes. Top the jicama with the fried eggs and serve immediately.

Zucchini Egg Bowl

This is a simple, delicious and super quick recipe for breakfast.

MAKES: 2 servings
PREPARATION TIME: 15 minutes
COOKING TIME: 4 minutes

Ingredients

1 large Zucchini, spiralized
Sea Salt, to taste
Freshly Ground Black Pepper, to taste
1½ tablespoons Extra Virgin Olive Oil
1 tablespoon Tamari
4 Organic Eggs
1 tablespoon Fresh Parsley, chopped

Directions

1. In a large frying pan, heat the remaining oil on a low heat. Carefully crack the eggs into the pan and spoon the hot oil over the whites until set. Spoon the oil over yolks, but only a couple of times as the yolks should be runny. Cook for about 3 to 4 minutes.
2. Meanwhile, place the spiralized zucchini in a microwave safe bowl. Sprinkle with salt and black pepper. Microwave on high for about 1 minute. Drizzle with ½ tablespoon of oil and tamari. Microwave for 1 minute more. Transfer the zucchini to a large serving plate.
3. Top the zucchini with the fried eggs, garnish with parsley and serve.

Gingery Zucchini Soup

This is a warm, filling, flavorful and delicious soup. This dish will be ideal for when you have a cold.

MAKES: 2 servings
PREPARATION TIME: 10 minutes
COOKING TIME: 15 minutes

Ingredients

1 tablespoon Extra Virgin Olive Oil
1 teaspoon Garlic, minced
1 tablespoon Fresh Ginger, minced
3-4 cups Homemade Vegetable Broth
2 tablespoons Coconut Aminos
3 teaspoons Coconut Vinegar
1 cup Kale, trimmed and chopped
2 Organic Large Eggs, beaten
1 Medium Zucchini, spiralized
1 Scallion, chopped
Sea Salt, to taste
Freshly Ground Black Pepper, to taste

Directions

1. In a large soup pan, heat the oil on a medium heat. Sauté the garlic and ginger for about 1 minute. Add the broth, coconut aminos and vinegar, and bring to the boil. Cook for about 4 to 5 minutes. Add the kale and cook for a further 4 to 5 minutes.
2. Slowly, add the beaten eggs, stirring continuously. Stir in the zucchini, scallion and seasoning. Cook for 3 to 4 minutes before serving hot.

Easy Egg Spree

This recipe makes an affordable and delicious meal. Enjoy the short cooking time as you also enjoy this delicious meal.

MAKES: 2 servings
PREPARATION TIME: 15 minutes
COOKING TIME: 10 minutes

Ingredients

2 tablespoons Extra Virgin Olive Oil
1 medium Sweet Potato, peeled and spiralized
1 medium Zucchini, spiralized
4 Organic Eggs
Sea Salt, to taste
Freshly Ground Black Pepper, to taste

Directions

1. In a large skillet, heat 1½ tablespoons of oil on a medium heat. Add the spiralized sweet potato and cook for 3 to 4 minutes. Add the zucchini and cook for 2 to 3 minutes.
2. Make a well in the center of the vegetables and pour the remaining oil into the well. Carefully crack the eggs into the well. Cover the skillet and cook for 2 to 3 minutes, or until the eggs are cooked to your satisfaction.
3. Sprinkle with salt and black pepper before serving.

MEATLESS RECIPES

Creamy Squash Delight

This is a simple recipe with a wonderful taste. The combination of coconut milk and fresh herbs worked very nicely in this dish.

MAKES: 4 servings
PREPARATION TIME: 15 minutes
(plus time to marinate)

Ingredients

1½ pounds Summer Squash, spiralized
Sea Salt, to taste
¼ cup Organic Coconut Milk
2 tablespoons Fresh Lemon juice
2 tablespoons Extra Virgin Olive Oil
1 Garlic Clove, minced
3 tablespoons minced Parsley Leaves
3 tablespoons minced Basil Leaves
3 tablespoons minced Tarragon Leaves
Freshly Ground Black Pepper, to taste
¼ cup Walnuts, chopped

Directions

1. Place the spiralized squash into a large colander and sprinkle with salt. Arrange the colander over a large bowl. Set aside for at least 15 to 20 minutes. Gently squeeze the squash and pat dry with a paper towel. Transfer the squash into a large serving bowl.
2. Add the remaining ingredients into a food processor, except for the black pepper and walnuts, and pulse until smooth. Pour the herb mixture over the squash. Sprinkle with salt and black pepper and toss to coat well.
3. Top with walnuts and serve.

Yellow Squash Tomatoes

Yellow squash with tomatoes is an easy way to enjoy fresh summer squash. This dish combination makes these squash noodles really delicious.

MAKES: 4 servings
PREPARATION TIME: 15 minutes

Ingredients

1 pound Yellow Squash, spiralized
1½ cups Cherry Tomatoes, halved
¼ cup Organic Coconut Milk
2 tablespoons Extra Virgin Olive Oil
1 Garlic Clove, minced
1 cup Fresh Basil Leaves, chopped
Sea Salt, to taste
Freshly Ground Black Pepper, to taste

Directions

1. Place the spiralized squash and tomatoes into a large serving bowl.
2. In a food processor, add the remaining ingredients, except for the salt and black pepper, and pulse until smooth. Pour the basil mixture over the vegetables. Sprinkle with black pepper and salt, toss to coat well before serving immediately.

Zucchini Green Rainbow

Enjoy a great raw noodle dish with a beautiful green color. You will find these noodles to be energizing!

MAKES: 4 servings
PREPARATION TIME: 15 minutes

Ingredients

4 Zucchinis, spiralized
1 cup Mixed Vegetables (Spinach, Kale, Arugula)
2 tablespoons freshly chopped Basil Leaves,
2 Garlic Cloves
2 tablespoons Fresh Lemon juice
3 tablespoons Extra Virgin Olive Oil
Sea Salt, to taste
Freshly Ground Black Pepper, to taste
¼ cup Walnuts, chopped

Directions

1. Place the spiralized zucchini into a large serving bowl.
2. In a food processor, add the remaining ingredients, except for the salt, black pepper and walnuts, and pulse until smooth. Pour the vegetable mixture over the zucchini. Sprinkle with black pepper and salt, and thoroughly mix the dish.
3. Top with walnuts and serve.

Hearty Zucchini Broccoli

This is a great casual and satisfying meal. This dish will satisfy the taste buds of all who taste it.

MAKES: 4 servings
PREPARATION TIME: 15 minutes

Ingredients

3-4 Zucchinis, spiralized
2 Garlic Cloves, minced
½ cup Broccoli Florets, chopped
2 cups Fresh Kale, trimmed and torn
½ cup freshly chopped Cilantro Leaves
2 tablespoons Fresh Lemon juice
Sea Salt, to taste
Freshly Ground Black Pepper, to taste

Directions

1. Place spiralized zucchini into a large serving bowl.
2. In a food processor, add the remaining ingredients, except for the salt and black pepper, and pulse until smooth. Pour the kale mixture over the zucchini. Sprinkle with black pepper and salt, and toss to coat well before serving immediately.

Tangy Zucchini Fiesta

This easy recipe nicely combines zucchini noodles and vegetables with a refreshingly tangy sauce.

MAKES: 4 servings
PREPARATION TIME: 20 minutes

Ingredients

4 Zucchinis, spiralized
¼ cup Fresh Baby Spinach
¼ cup Fresh Baby Kale
2 tablespoons Black Olives, pitted and halved
2 tablespoons Green Olives, pitted and halved
1 Garlic Clove, minced
½ teaspoon Lemon Zest, freshly grated
2 tablespoons Fresh Lemon juice
2 tablespoons Extra Virgin Olive Oil
Sea Salt, to taste
Freshly Ground Black Pepper, to taste
¼ cup Almonds, chopped

Directions

1. In a large serving bowl, mix together the spiralized zucchini, spinach, kale and olives.
2. In another bowl, mix together the remaining ingredients, except for the almonds. Pour the lemon mixture over the vegetables and toss to coat well.
3. Top with almonds and serve immediately.

Zoodle Spinach Spirals

Garden fresh zucchini and carrot easily transforms into a special meal with just a few basic ingredients.

MAKES: 4 servings
PREPARATION TIME: 15 minutes

Ingredients

2 large Zucchinis, peeled and spiralized
2 large Carrots, peeled and spiralized
3 cups fresh Spinach, torn
3 Garlic Cloves, minced
¼ cup Raw Pumpkin Seeds
3 tablespoons Extra Virgin Olive Oil
Sea Salt, to taste
Freshly Ground Black Pepper, to taste

Directions

1. Place the spiralized zucchini and carrots into a large serving bowl.
2. In a food processor, add the remaining ingredients and pulse until smooth. Pour the spinach mixture over the vegetables, mix the dish thoroughly and serve immediately.

Sesame Carrot Noodles

This dish is one of the best combinations of herb sauce with raw carrot noodles. This meal is delicious and healthy plus packed with beta carotene and vitamins.

MAKES: 2 servings
PREPARATION TIME: 15 minutes

Ingredients

2 large Carrots, peeled and spiralized
1 medium Green Bell Pepper, seeded and chopped
1 teaspoon Fresh Ginger, grated
1 Garlic Clove, minced
½ cup Freshly chopped Basil Leaves
2 tablespoons Extra Virgin Olive Oil
1 tablespoon Fresh Lemon juice
1 teaspoon Tamari
2 tablespoons Sesame Seeds

Directions

1. Place the spiralized carrots and bell pepper into a large serving bowl.
2. In a food processor, add the remaining ingredients, except for the sesame seeds, and pulse until smooth. Pour the basil mixture over the carrots and toss to coat well.
3. Top with sesame seeds and serve.

Sweet & Spicy Curls

This raw pasta is perfect for a time when you need a fresh, satisfying dish without spending a lot of time cooking.

MAKES: 2 servings
PREPARATION TIME: 20 minutes

Ingredients

1 Zucchini, peeled and spiralized
1 Cucumber, peeled and spiralized
¼ cup Almond Butter
1 tablespoon Fresh Lemon juice
1 tablespoon Raw Honey
1 tablespoon Tamari
2 tablespoons Water
⅛ teaspoon Cayenne Pepper, crushed
Sea Salt, to taste
Freshly Ground Black Pepper, to taste
2 tablespoons Almonds, chopped

Directions

1. Place the spiralized vegetables into a large colander. Arrange the colander over a large bowl. Set aside for at least 15 to 20 minutes. Gently squeeze the vegetables and pat dry with a paper towel. Transfer the vegetables into a large serving bowl.
2. In another bowl, mix together the remaining ingredients, except for the almonds. Pour the honey mixture over the vegetables and toss to coat well.
3. Top with almonds and serve immediately.

Sweet & Sour Cucumbers

This is an absolutely gorgeous and refreshing dish for the whole family. This recipe adds a great twist to regular cucumber.

MAKES: 4 servings
PREPARATION TIME: 20 minutes (plus time to refrigerate)

Ingredients

3 large Cucumbers, peeled and spiralized
1 Red Onion, sliced thinly
¼ cup Fresh Lemon juice
2 tablespoons Filtered Water
2 teaspoons Raw Honey
Sea Salt, to taste
Freshly Ground Black Pepper, to taste
2 teaspoons Sesame Seeds

Directions

1. Place the spiralized cucumbers and onion into a large serving bowl.
2. In another bowl, mix together the remaining ingredients, except for the sesame seeds. Pour the honey mixture over the vegetables and toss to coat well. Cover and refrigerate to chill.
3. Top with sesame seeds and serve.

Sweet & Sour Roasted Beets

This sweet and sour sauce nicely compliments the taste of the beets and crunch of the almonds.

MAKES: 4 servings
PREPARATION TIME: 20 minutes
COOKING TIME: 5 minutes

Ingredients

4 medium Beets, peeled and spiralized
2½ tablespoons Extra Virgin Olive Oil
Sea Salt, to taste
Freshly Ground Black Pepper, to taste
1 tablespoons Onion, minced
1 Garlic Clove, minced
2 tablespoons Almond Butter
2½ tablespoons Raw Honey
2½ tablespoons Fresh Lemon juice
¼ cup Almonds, chopped

Directions

1. Preheat the oven to 400 degrees F and grease a baking sheet. Place the spiralized beets onto the prepared baking sheet and drizzle with ½ tablespoon of oil. Sprinkle with salt and black pepper and roast for about 5 minutes before removing the baking sheet from the oven. Transfer the beets into a serving bowl.
2. In a food processor, add the remaining ingredients, except for the almonds, and pulse until smooth. Pour the honey mixture over the beets and toss to coat well.
3. Top with the almonds and serve immediately.

Creamy Coated Cucumber

This cucumber pasta with creamy avocado sauce is very light and hearty. This will become a favorite raw vegetable noodle recipe.

MAKES: 2 servings
PREPARATION TIME: 20 minutes

Ingredients

2 large Cucumbers, peeled and spiralized
1 Ripe Avocado, peeled, pitted and sliced
2 Garlic Cloves, minced
1 Plum Tomato, chopped
1 tablespoon Scallion, chopped
1 tablespoon Fresh Lemon juice
Sea Salt, to taste
Freshly Ground Black Pepper, to taste

Directions

1. Place the spiralized cucumbers into a large serving bowl.
2. In a food processor, add the remaining ingredients and pulse until smooth. Pour the avocado mixture over the cucumbers and toss to coat well.
3. Serve immediately.

Velvety Cucumber Beets

This recipe, packed with great flavors, makes a perfect and light meal.

MAKES: 2 servings
PREPARATION TIME: 15 minutes

Ingredients

2 medium Beets, peeled and spiralized
1 large Cucumber, peeled and spiralized
1 large Ripe Avocado, peeled, pitted and chopped
2 Garlic Cloves, minced
¼ cup Hemp Seeds
1 tablespoon Tamari
1 tablespoon Walnut Oil
2 tablespoons Fresh Lemon juice
⅛ teaspoon Cayenne Pepper
Sea Salt, to taste
Freshly Ground Black Pepper, to taste

Directions

1. Place the spiralized beets and cucumbers into a large serving bowl.
2. In a food processor, add the remaining ingredients and pulse until smooth. Pour the avocado mixture over the vegetables. Toss to coat well and serve immediately.

Nutty Veggie Mix

Each bite of this dish is infused with the fresh flavors of carrot and beets, and the great taste of the fresh herbs.

MAKES: 4 servings
PREPARATION TIME: 20 minutes

Ingredients

2 large Carrots, peeled and spiralized
2 small Red Beets, peeled and spiralized
2 small Yellow Beets, peeled and spiralized
½ cup Walnuts, chopped
2 Garlic Cloves, minced
½ cup freshly chopped Parsley Leaves
¾ cup freshly chopped Basil Leaves
½ cup Walnut Oil
Sea Salt, to taste
Freshly Ground Black Pepper, to taste

Directions

1. Place the spiralized carrots and beets into a large serving bowl.
2. In a food processor, add ¼ cup walnuts and the remaining ingredients, and pulse until smooth. Pour the herb mixture over the vegetables and toss to coat well.
3. Top with the remaining walnuts and serve immediately.

Cucumber Asparagus Glee

The crisp asparagus spears and spinach is a perfect companion to the cucumber noodles in this recipe.

MAKES: 2 servings
PREPARATION TIME: 20 minutes
COOKING TIME: 3 minutes

Ingredients

1 Bunch Asparagus, trimmed and cut into 2-inch slices
1 cup Fresh Spinach, torn
2 Cucumbers, peeled and spiralized
1 teaspoon Fresh Ginger, grated
2 Scallions, chopped
2 tablespoons Extra Virgin Olive Oil
1½ tablespoons Tamari
⅛ teaspoon Cayenne Pepper
Sea Salt, to taste
Freshly Ground Black Pepper, to taste
2 tablespoons Sesame Seeds, toasted

Directions

1. In a pan of salted boiling water, add the asparagus and spinach and cook for 2 to 3 minutes. Drain and immediately place into a bowl of ice water. Immediately drain well.
2. In a large serving bowl, place the asparagus, spinach and spiralized cucumbers.
3. In another bowl, mix together the remaining ingredients, except for the sesame seeds. Pour the ginger mixture over the vegetables and toss to coat well. Top with

73

sesame seeds and serve immediately.

Buttered Sweet Potato

*This delicious dish is a great way for your little ones to enjoy
sweet potato. Enjoy this comforting and healthy dish.*

MAKES: 4 servings
PREPARATION TIME: 10 minutes
COOKING TIME: 8 minutes

Ingredients

*2 large Sweet Potatoes, peeled and spiralized
1 tablespoon Almond Butter
1 teaspoon Coconut Palm Sugar
½ teaspoon Ground Cinnamon*

Directions

1. Place the spiralized sweet potato into a steamer basket.
   Arrange the basket over a pan of boiling water and steam
   for 6 to 8 minutes, or until tender. Transfer the sweet
   potato into a serving bowl and let it cool slightly.
2. Stir in the butter and sprinkle with sugar and cinnamon
   before serving.

BEEF, PORK & LAMB RECIPES

Crunchy Steak Salad

This is a nutrient packed bowl of salad with mounds of gorgeous vegetables and delicious steak. These vegetables are really crunchy and oh so yummy!

MAKES: 4 servings
PREPARATION TIME: 20 minutes (plus time to marinate)
COOKING TIME: 18 minutes

Ingredients

For Steak
⅓ cup Coconut Aminos
1 tablespoon Fresh Lemon juice
Sea Salt, to taste
Freshly Ground Black Pepper, to taste
¾ pound Grass-Fed trimmed Sirloin Steak

For Veggies:
3 zucchinis, spiralized

1 medium Carrot, peeled and spiralized
1 Cucumber, spiralized
1 Red Bell Pepper, seeded and sliced thinly
2 Garlic Cloves
¼ cup Fresh Cilantro Leaves, minced
2 tablespoons Fresh Lemon Juice
3 tablespoons Extra Virgin Olive Oil
Sea Salt, to taste
Freshly Ground Black Pepper, to taste
1 teaspoon Sesame Seeds, toasted

Directions

1. For the steak, in a large bowl mix together all of the steak ingredients, except for the steak. Add the steak and generously coat with the marinade. Cover and refrigerate for at least 6 to 8 hours. Preheat the grill to a medium-high heat. Grill the steak for 5 to 6 minutes per side. Remove from the grill and transfer onto a cutting board. Set aside for 10 minutes. With a sharp knife slice the steak according to your preference.
2. Meanwhile, in a large serving bowl mix together the spiralized zucchini, carrot, cucumber and bell pepper. In another bowl, mix together the remaining ingredients, except for the sesame seeds. Pour the dressing over the vegetables and toss to coat.
3. Top the vegetables with the steak slices. Garnish with sesame seeds and serve.

Squash Beef Soup

This is a warm and comforting beef and yellow squash noodle soup. This recipe makes a wonderfully healthy and delicious soup that will leave you feeling light yet full.

MAKES: 2 servings
PREPARATION TIME: 15 minutes
COOKING TIME: 20 minutes

Ingredients

1 ½ tablespoons Extra Virgin Olive Oil
½ pound Grass-Fed NY Strip Steak, trimmed and cubed
Sea Salt, to taste
Freshly Ground Black Pepper, to taste
1 small Onion, chopped
1 Celery Stalk, chopped
2 teaspoons Garlic, minced
2 cups Baby Spinach
2 ½ cups Homemade Beef Broth
1 tablespoon Coconut Aminos
1 large Yellow Squash, spiralized
½ cup Scallions, chopped
1 tablespoon minced Parsley Leaves

Directions

1. In a large soup pan, heat the oil on a medium heat. Add the beef and sprinkle with the salt and black pepper. Cook for 2 to 3 minutes. Transfer the beef onto a plate.
2. In the same pan sauté the onion and celery for 4 to 5 minutes. Sauté the garlic for about 1 minute. Add the spinach and cook for a further 2 minutes. Add the broth

and coconut aminos and bring the pan to the boil. Reduce the heat and simmer for 5 minutes. Add the spiralized squash and beef, and cook for 2 to 3 minutes. Stir in the scallions and cook for 1 minute more.

3. Season with salt and black pepper. Remove the dish from the heat, garnish with parsley and serve immediately.

Zucchini Meatball Soup

This is an easy, simple, yet nourishing soup with the wonderful flavors of zucchini, beef and vegetables.

MAKES: 2 servings
PREPARATION TIME: 20 minutes
COOKING TIME: 30 minutes

Ingredients

For Meatballs
1 pound Grass-Fed Ground Beef (Extra Lean)
½ Red Onion, chopped
4-6 Black Olives, pitted and chopped
1 small Red Bell Pepper, seeded and chopped
3 Garlic Cloves, chopped finely
2 tablespoons Freshly chopped Parsley
¼ cup Coconut Flour
1 Organic Egg, beaten
½ teaspoon Cayenne Pepper
Sea Salt, to taste
Freshly Ground Black Pepper, to taste
1 tablespoon Extra Virgin Olive Oil

For Soup
2 tablespoons Extra Virgin Olive Oil
1 medium Onion, chopped
2 Celery Stalks, chopped
1 Carrot, chopped finely
2 Garlic Cloves, minced
7-8 cups Homemade Beef Broth
1½ cups Kale, trimmed and chopped
1 teaspoon Dried Oregano, crushed

Sea Salt, to taste
Freshly Ground Black Pepper, to taste
2-3 large Zucchinis, spiralized
1 tablespoon Fresh Lemon juice

Directions

1. For meatballs, in a large bowl mix together all of the ingredients, except for the oil. Make your desired size balls from the mixture. In a large skillet, heat the oil on a medium heat and add the meatballs in batches. Cook for 3 to 4 minutes, or until golden brown. Transfer the meatballs onto a plate and set aside.
2. For the soup, in a large soup pan heat the oil on a medium heat. Sauté the onion, celery and carrot for 4 to 5 minutes before sautéing the garlic for 1 minute. Add the broth and bring to the boil before reducing the heat to medium-low. Simmer for 3 to 4 minutes before gently adding the meatballs. Cover and simmer for about 10 minutes. Stir in the kale, oregano and seasoning, and cook for 2 to 3 minutes.
3. Stir in the spiralized zucchini and cook for 2 to 3 minutes more. Stir in lemon juice, remove the pan from the heat and serve immediately.

Saucy Zucchini Steak

This is an amazingly delicious and satisfying dish that is quickly prepared. This dish is perfect for family dinners.

MAKES: 4 servings
PREPARATION TIME: 15 minutes
COOKING TIME: 18 minutes

Ingredients

1½ tablespoons Extra Virgin Olive Oil
1 pound Grass-Fed Skirt Steak, trimmed and sliced thinly
Sea Salt, to taste
Freshly Ground Black Pepper, to taste
½ teaspoon Arrowroot Powder
¼ cup Homemade Vegetable Broth
1 Garlic Clove, minced
1 cup Organic Coconut Milk
½ teaspoon Coconut Aminos
3-4 Zucchinis, spiralized
2 tablespoons minced Parsley Leaves

Directions

1. In a large skillet, heat 1 tablespoon of oil on a medium-high heat. Add the steak and sprinkle with salt and black pepper. Cook the steak for about 5 minutes, turning once after 2½ minutes. Transfer the steak onto a plate.
2. In the same skillet, heat the remaining oil on a medium heat. Meanwhile, in a bowl mix together the arrowroot and broth. Sauté the garlic in the preheated skillet for 1 minute. Pour in the broth mixture and cook for 1 minute whilst stirring continuously. Add the coconut milk and coconut aminos and season with salt and black pepper.

Cook the dish for about 10 minutes and stir it occasionally. Stir in the zucchini and cook for a further 2 minutes.

3. Transfer the zucchini mixture onto a serving plate. Top with the steak slices, garnish with parsley and serve.

Beefy Squash Greens

This is a mild spicy dish of marinated steak and sautéed fresh greens over summer squash noodles. In this recipe the beef combines nicely with squash and sautéed greens.

MAKES: 4 servings
PREPARATION TIME: 15 minutes (plus time to marinate)
COOKING TIME: 25 minutes

Ingredients

For Steak
2 Garlic Cloves, minced
1 teaspoon Fresh Ginger, minced
¼ teaspoon Red Chili Powder
Sea Salt, to taste
Freshly Ground Black Pepper, to taste
2 tablespoons Coconut Vinegar
1 pound Grass-Fed Flank Steak, trimmed and sliced thinly
1 tablespoon Extra Virgin Olive Oil

For Vegetables
1 tablespoon Extra Virgin Olive Oil
1 small White Onion, chopped
1 teaspoon Fresh Ginger, minced
2 Garlic Cloves, minced
1 cup Carrots, peeled and chopped very finely
¼ cup Homemade Beef Broth
1 tablespoon Coconut Vinegar
½ tablespoon Dried Basil, crushed
Sea Salt, to taste
Freshly Ground Black Pepper, to taste
4 cups Mixed Greens (Arugula, Spinach, Kale for example)

3 Summer Squashes, spiralized
¼ cup Scallions, sliced thinly

Directions

1. For the steak, in a large bowl mix together all of the ingredients, except for the steak and oil. Add the steak and generously coat with the marinade. Cover and refrigerate for at least 20 to 24 hours. In a large skillet, heat the oil on a medium heat. Remove beef from marinade and discard any excess marinade. Cook the beef for about 4 to 5 minutes. Transfer the beef onto a plate and set aside.
2. For the vegetables, in the same skillet heat the oil on a medium heat. Sauté the onion for 4 to 5 minutes before sautéing the ginger and garlic for 1 minute. Stir in the carrots and cook for 3 to 4 minutes. Add the broth, vinegar, basil and seasoning and bring to the boil. Stir in the greens, reduce the heat and simmer for 4 to 5 minutes. Stir in the squash and cook for 4 to 5 minutes.
3. Transfer the squash mixture onto a serving plate. Top with the steak slices, garnish with scallions and serve.

Rutabaga Spiced Beef

*This recipe makes a divine meal for the whole family. Tomatoes
and spices add a wonderful flavor to this dish.*

MAKES: 4 servings
PREPARATION TIME: 15 minutes
COOKING TIME: 4 hours

Ingredients

1 tablespoon Extra Virgin Coconut Oil
1 pound cubed, Grass-Fed Stewing Beef
Sea Salt, to taste
Freshly Ground Black Pepper, to taste
2 Celery Stalks, chopped
1 large Onion, chopped
2 Garlic Cloves, minced
10-12 Fresh Tomatoes, finely chopped
5-6 Fresh Tomatoes, pureed
1½ cups Water
¼ teaspoon Cayenne Pepper
1 tablespoon Ground Cinnamon
¼ teaspoon Ground Cloves
1 tablespoon Dried Oregano, crushed
1 tablespoon dried Thyme, crushed
6 small Rutabagas, spiralized

Directions

1. In a large pan, add the beef to the oil heated on a
   medium-high-heat, and sprinkle with salt and black
   pepper. Cook for about 4 to 5 minutes, or until golden
   brown. Transfer the beef onto a plate.

2. In the same skillet, add the celery and onion and sauté for 4 to 5 minutes before sautéing the garlic for 1 minute. Add the tomatoes and cook for 1 to 2 minutes, crushing them. Except for the rutabagas, add the beef and remaining ingredients to the skillet and bring to boil before reducing the heat and simmering, covered, for 3 to 4 hours.
3. Meanwhile, place the spiralized rutabagas in a steamer basket and sprinkle with salt. Set the steamer basket over a pan of boiling water and steam for 4 to 5 minutes. On a serving plate place steamed the rutabagas. Top with beef mixture and serve.

Sweet Beef & Veggies

This recipe is perfect for a delicious weeknight dinner. This dish is filled with the healthy nutrients of beef, sweet potatoes and tomatoes.

MAKES: 4 servings
PREPARATION TIME: 20 minutes
COOKING TIME: 52 minutes

Ingredients

1½ tablespoons Coconut Oil, Extra Virgin
1 large Onion, chopped
1 cup Celery, chopped
2 Carrots, peeled and chopped
1 cup Green Bell Pepper, seeded and chopped
1 Pound Grass-Fed Stewing Beef, trimmed and cubed
3-4 Fresh Tomatoes, chopped finely
1½ cups Homemade Tomato Puree
½ cup Homemade Beef Broth
1 tablespoon Dried Basil, crushed
Sea Salt, to taste
Freshly Ground Black Pepper, to taste
2 large Sweet Potatoes, peeled and spiralized
2 tablespoons chopped Scallions

Directions

1. In a large skillet, heat the oil on a medium heat. Sauté the onion, celery, carrots and bell peppers for 4 to 5 minutes. Add the beef and, whilst occasionally stirring, cook for about 10 minutes.
2. Add the tomatoes and cook for 1 to 2 minutes, crushing

them. Add the remaining ingredients, except for the sweet potato, and bring to the boil and continue to cook for about 15 minutes (add a little water if needed). Next, reduce the heat and allow simmering while covered, for about 10-15 minutes. Stir in the spiralized sweet potato and cook for 8 to 10 minutes.

3. Garnish with scallions and serve.

Lemony Beef Zucchini

This is a wonderfully tasty dish which nicely combines zucchinis with beef and kale. The garnishing of sesame seeds adds a nice kick to this meal.

MAKES: 2 servings
PREPARATION TIME: 20 minutes (plus time to marinate)
COOKING TIME: 15 minutes

Ingredients

For Beef
¼ cup Coconut Aminos
1 tablespoon Fresh Lemon juice
1 tablespoon Extra Virgin Olive Oil
Sea Salt, to taste
Freshly Ground Black Pepper, to taste
½ pound trimmed, Grass-Fed Sirloin Steak

For Vegetables
1 tablespoon Extra Virgin Olive Oil
1 large Onion, chopped
1 Celery Rib, chopped
1 Garlic Clove, minced
1 teaspoon Fresh Ginger, minced
1 Jalapeño Pepper, chopped
¼ cup Coconut Aminos
Sea Salt, to taste
Freshly Ground Black Pepper, to taste
2 medium Zucchinis, spiralized
1 cup fresh Kale, trimmed and chopped
1 tablespoon Black Sesame Seeds

Directions

1. For the steak, in a large bowl mix together all of the ingredients, except for the steak. Thinly slice the steak and generously coat with the marinade before covering with cling film and refrigerating for at least 2 to 3 hours. Heat a large non-stick skillet on a medium heat. Add the beef with marinade and cook for 4 to 5 minutes before removing from the heat and setting aside.
2. For the vegetables, in another large skillet heat the oil on a medium heat. Sauté the onion and celery for 3 to 4 minutes. Add the garlic, ginger and jalapeño pepper and sauté for 1 minute. Pour in the coconut aminos and cook for 1 to 2 minutes. Stir in the seasoning, zucchini and kale, and cook for 2 to 3 minutes more.
3. Place the zucchini mixture on a serving plate. Top with the beef, garnish with sesame seeds and serve.

Sweet Potato Minced Beef

This is one of the best warming dishes prepared for dinnertime.
This recipe is also a great way to make beef healthier.

MAKES: 4 servings
PREPARATION TIME: 15 minutes
COOKING TIME: 30 minutes

Ingredients

2 large Sweet Potatoes, peeled and spiralized
1 tablespoon Extra Virgin Olive Oil
1 White Onion, chopped
2 Garlic Cloves, minced
1 Pound Grass-Fed Ground Beef (Extra Lean)
¼ teaspoon Red Chili Powder
Sea Salt, to taste
Freshly Ground Black Pepper, to taste
½ cup Homemade Beef Broth
3 cups Fresh Tomatoes, crushed
2 Red Bell Peppers, seeded and chopped
1 tablespoon Mixed Died Herbs (thyme, oregano, marjoram,
basil), crushed
¼ cup minced Cilantro Leaves

Directions

1. In a large pan of boiling water, add the spiralized sweet potato and cook for 4 to 5 minutes before draining and setting aside.
2. In a large skillet, heat the oil on a medium heat. Sauté the onion for 8 to 9 minutes before sautéing the garlic for 1 minute. Add the beef and sprinkle with chili powder, salt and black pepper. Cook, stirring occasionally, for about 10 minutes. Add the broth, tomatoes, bell pepper and

herbs and cook, stirring occasionally, for 5 to 10 minutes.
3. On a serving plate place the sweet potato. Top with the beef mixture, garnish with cilantro and serve.

Cabbage & Beef Fete

This is a family friendly recipe that will surely satisfy the taste buds. This delicious dish contains a dense source of healthy nutrients.

MAKES: 4 servings
PREPARATION TIME: 15 minutes
COOKING TIME: 30 minutes

Ingredients

1 tablespoon Extra Virgin Olive Oil
1 Yellow Onion, chopped
2 large Red Bell Peppers, seeded and chopped
1 Pound Grass-Fed Ground Beef (Extra Lean)
1 teaspoon Dried thyme, crushed
1 medium Head Cabbage, spiralized
3 cups Fresh Roma Tomatoes, pureed
Sea Salt, to taste
Freshly Ground Black Pepper, to taste
⅓ Cup Fresh Parsley, chopped

Directions

1. In a large skillet, heat the oil on a medium heat. Add the onion and bell peppers and sauté for about 4 to 5 minutes. Add the beef and thyme and cook for 8 to 10 minutes.
2. Stir in the spiralized cabbage, tomato puree and seasoning. Reduce the heat, cover and simmer for 10 to15 minutes.
3. Garnish with parsley and serve.

Garlicky Zucchini with Baked Meatballs

The addition of black olives adds a wonderful trick to this dish. This delicious dish will amuse everyone present at the dining table.

MAKES: 4 servings
PREPARATION TIME: 15 minutes
COOKING TIME: 15 minutes

Ingredients

For Meatballs
1 pound Grass-Fed Ground Beef (Extra Lean)
¼ cup Fresh Rosemary, chopped
¼ teaspoon Cayenne Pepper
Sea Salt, to taste
Freshly Ground Black Pepper, to taste

For Zucchini
1 tablespoon Extra Virgin Olive Oil
10-12 Garlic Cloves, minced
1 cup Red Bell Pepper, seeded and chopped
1 cup Black Olives, pitted and sliced
3-4 Large Zucchinis, spiralized
½ cup minced Cilantro Leaves

Directions

1. Preheat the oven to 400 degrees F and line a cookie sheet with parchment paper. For the meatballs, in a large bowl mix together all of the ingredients. Make your desired size balls from the mixture. Arrange the balls on the prepared cookie sheet in a single layer and bake for 12 to 15 minutes.

95

2. Meanwhile, in a large skillet heat the oil on a medium heat. Sauté the garlic and bell pepper for 4 to 5 minutes. Add the olives and cook for a further 2 minutes. Stir in the zucchini and cilantro, and cook for 2 to 3 minutes more.
3. Place the zucchini mixture onto a serving plate. Top with the meatballs and sauce before serving.

Sesame Shredded Cabbage

This cabbage and beef dish is easy and quick to prepare. The cabbage used in this dish pairs really well with the beef and sweet and sour sauce.

MAKES: 4 servings
PREPARATION TIME: 15 minutes
COOKING TIME: 22 minutes

Ingredients

1 tablespoon + 1 teaspoon Coconut Oil
1 pound Grass-Fed Ground Beef (Extra Lean)
1 medium Head Cabbage, spiralized
⅓ Cup Almond Butter
3 tablespoons Coconut Aminos
2 tablespoons Coconut Vinegar
1 tablespoon Organic Honey
1 tablespoon Sesame Seeds, toasted

Directions

1. In a large non-stick skillet, heat 1 teaspoon oil on a medium-high heat. Add the beef and cook for 4 to 5 minutes. Spread the spiralized cabbage evenly over the beef. Cover and cook for about 10 minutes before uncovering and cooking for 5 minutes more.
2. In a small bowl, mix together the remaining ingredients, except for the sesame seeds. Pour the butter mixture over the spiralized cabbage. Cook for a further 2 minutes, or until heated completely.
3. Garnish with sesame seeds and serve.

Olives & Zucchini Lean

This is a quick, easy and, of course, healthy and tempting recipe.
This dish is suitable for family and friends gatherings.

MAKES: 2 servings
PREPARATION TIME: 20 minutes
COOKING TIME: 25 minutes

Ingredients

1 tablespoon Extra Virgin Olive Oil
¼ cup White Onion, chopped
1 Garlic Clove, minced
½ pound Grass-Fed Ground Beef (Extra Lean)
1 teaspoon Dried Thyme, crushed
Sea Salt, to taste
Freshly Ground Black Pepper, to taste
¼ cup Homemade Beef Broth
2 large Tomatoes, seeded and chopped
3 Zucchinis, spiralized
1 cup Black Olives, pitted and halved
1 large Avocado, peeled, pitted and cubed

Directions

1. In a large skillet, heat the oil on a medium heat. Sauté the onion for 4 to 5 minutes before sautéing the garlic for 1 minute. Add the beef and sprinkle with thyme, salt and black pepper. Cook for about 10 minutes whilst stirring occasionally.
2. Add the broth and cook for 3 to 4 minutes. Add the tomatoes and cook for 1 to 2 minutes whilst stirring occasionally.
3. Stir in the remaining ingredients and cook for 2 to 3 minutes.

Squash Spaghetti & Meatballs

This is a delicious combination of spiralized squash with meatballs in sauce. The addition of chia seeds in the meatballs makes them very succulent and tasty.

MAKES: 4 servings
PREPARATION TIME: 20 minutes
COOKING TIME: 40 minutes

Ingredients

For Meatballs
1 pound Grass-Fed Ground Beef (Extra Lean)
2 tablespoons Chia Seeds
2 Garlic Cloves, minced
2 tablespoons Homemade Tomato Puree
½ tablespoon Fresh Thyme, minced
½ tablespoon Fresh Oregano, minced
Sea Salt, to taste
Freshly Ground Black Pepper, to taste
2 teaspoons Extra Virgin Olive Oil

For Sauce
½ tablespoon Extra Virgin Olive Oil
1 medium White Onion, chopped
1 Garlic Clove, minced
2 tablespoons Fresh Thyme, chopped
½ cup Homemade Beef Broth
2 tablespoons Fresh Lemon juice
1½ cups Fresh Tomatoes, chopped finely
1½ cups Homemade Tomato puree
Sea Salt, to taste
Freshly Ground Black Pepper, to taste
3 large Yellow Squash, spiralized

Directions

1. For meatballs, in a large bowl mix together all of the ingredients, except for the oil. Set aside for at least 10 minutes. Make your desired size balls from the mixture. In a large skillet, heat the oil on a medium heat. Add the meatballs and cook for 3 to 4 minutes. Transfer onto a plate and set aside.
2. For the sauce, in the same skillet heat the oil on a medium heat. Sauté the onion for 4 to 5 minutes. Add the garlic and thyme and sauté for 1 minute. Add the broth and lemon juice and cook, stirring, for 1 minute. Add the remaining ingredients, except for the squash, and cook for 15 to 20 minutes. Stir in the meatballs and reduce the heat to medium-low. Cook for 5 to 10 minutes until cooked.
3. Place the spiralized squash onto a serving plate. Top with the meatballs and sauce before serving.

Roasted Lamb & Veggies

This dish is a perfect combination of healthy baked lamb cutlets with vegetables. The raw vegetables present a wonderful base to the lamb cutlets.

MAKES: 4 servings
PREPARATION TIME: 20 minutes
COOKING TIME: 20 minutes

Ingredients

For Lamb Cutlets

8 Grass-Fed Lamb Cutlets, trimmed
½ tablespoon Extra Virgin Olive Oil
1 tablespoon Fresh Rosemary, chopped
2 tablespoons minced Basil Leaves
Sea Salt, to taste
Freshly Ground Black Pepper, to taste

For Vegetables

1 large Cucumber, spiralized and pat dried
1 large Carrot, peeled and spiralized
1 Avocado, peeled, pitted and cubed
2 cups Fresh Baby Spinach
1 cup Cherry Tomatoes, halved
2 tablespoons Extra Virgin Olive Oil
2 tablespoons Fresh Lime juice
1 Garlic Clove, minced
3 tablespoons minced Cilantro Leaves
Sea Salt, to taste
Freshly Ground Black Pepper, to taste

Directions

1. Preheat the oven to 425 degrees F and grease a roasting

pan. Arrange the lamb cutlets in the prepared roasting pan and drizzle with oil. Generously sprinkle with the herbs and seasoning. Roast for about 20 minutes, turning once after 10 minutes.

2. Meanwhile, in a large serving bowl place the vegetables. In another bowl, mix together the remaining ingredients and pour the dressing over the vegetables and mix thoroughly.

3. Top with roasted cutlets and serve.

Zucchini Lamb Chops

This is a recipe for quick pan-seared lamb chops with freshly spiralized zucchini. This simple recipe makes quite a delicious and healthy meal.

MAKES: 4 servings
PREPARATION TIME: 20 minutes
COOKING TIME: 8 minutes

Ingredients

2 tablespoons Extra Virgin Olive Oil
1 Garlic Clove, minced
8 Grass-Fed Lamb Chops, trimmed
Sea Salt, to taste
Freshly Ground Black Pepper, to taste
3 large Zucchinis, spiralized
1 tablespoon Fresh Lime juice
½ cup Fresh Basil, chopped

Directions

1. In a large skillet, heat ½ tablespoon of oil on a medium-high heat. Sauté the garlic for 1 minute. Add the chops and sprinkle with salt and black pepper. Cook for about 6 minutes, turning once after 3 minutes. Transfer the chops onto a plate.
2. In the same skillet, heat the remaining oil on a medium-high heat. Add the spiralized zucchini and sprinkle with a little salt and black pepper. Sauté for about 1 to 2 minutes. Stir in lime juice and basil before removing the pan from the heat.
3. Place the zucchini mixture onto a serving plate. Top with the chops and serve.

Mixed Veggie Lamb Chops

This recipe is a perfect and beautiful combination of roasted vegetables with grilled lamb chops. This is could turn out to be a hit recipe for all who tries it.

MAKES: 4 servings
PREPARATION TIME: 25 minutes (plus time to marinate)
COOKING TIME: 20 minutes

Ingredients

For Lamb Chops
1 Onion, finely chopped
4 Garlic Cloves, minced
2 tablespoons Fresh Lemon juice
Sea Salt, to taste
Freshly Ground Black Pepper, to taste
8 Grass-Fed Lamb Chops, trimmed

For Vegetables
1 small Sweet potato, peeled and spiralized
1 medium Carrot, peeled and spiralized
1 medium Yellow Squash, spiralized
1 medium Zucchini, spiralized
1 small Orange Bell Pepper, seeded and sliced thinly
1 small Red Bell Pepper, seeded and sliced thinly
3 tablespoons Extra Virgin Olive Oil
1 tablespoon Dried Thyme, crushed
Sea Salt, to taste
Freshly Ground Black Pepper, to taste

Directions

1. For the chops, in a bowl mix together all of the ingredients, except for the chops. Add the chops and

generously coat with the marinade. Cover and refrigerate for at least 3 to 4 hours.

2. Preheat the oven to 400 degrees F and grease a large baking sheet. Mix together all of the vegetables, oil, thyme and seasoning in a large bowl. Arrange the vegetables in the prepared baking sheet in a thin layer. Roast for about 20 minutes, tossing once after 10 minutes.

3. Meanwhile, preheat the grill to a medium-high heat. Remove the chops from the marinade, shake off any excess marinade, and grill for about 6 minutes, turning once after 3 minutes.

4. Place the roasted vegetables on a serving plate. Top with the grilled chops and serve.

Zucchini Lamb Muffins

This meal combines delicious ground lamb muffins with a beautifully looking spiralized zucchini. This dish is packed with great flavors!

MAKES: 4 servings
PREPARATION TIME: 20 minutes
COOKING TIME: 20 minutes

Ingredients

For Lamb Muffins
1 pound Grass-Fed Ground Extra Lean Lamb
¼ cup White Onion, chopped
1 Garlic Clove, minced
1 large Organic Egg, beaten
3 tablespoons Almond Flour
½ teaspoon Ground Cinnamon
¼ teaspoon Cayenne Pepper
Sea Salt, to taste
Freshly Ground Black Pepper, to taste

For Zucchini
4-5 large Zucchinis, spiralized
Sea Salt, to taste
Freshly Ground Black Pepper, to taste
2 cups Fresh Kale
½ cup Fresh Basil, chopped
1 Garlic Clove, minced
½ cup Walnuts, chopped
1 tablespoon Fresh Lime juice
¼-½ Cup Homemade Vegetable Broth

Directions

1. Preheat the oven to 375 degrees F and line a 12 cup muffin pan with paper liners. In a large bowl mix together all of the muffin ingredients. Make 12 even sized balls from the mixture. Place the balls into the muffin cups and bake for about 20 minutes.
2. Meanwhile, place the spiralized zucchini into a microwave safe bowl. Sprinkle with salt and black pepper and microwave on high for about 2 minutes. Transfer the zucchini onto a large serving plate. In a food processor, add the kale, basil, garlic, walnuts, lime juice, broth, salt and black pepper and pulse until smooth. Pour the kale mixture over the zucchini and gently toss to coat.
3. Top with the lamb muffins and serve.

Sweet Pork Soup

This is a winter soup that is hearty and fulfilling. You may find that this soup is also loved by your kids.

MAKES: 4 servings
PREPARATION TIME: 25 minutes
COOKING TIME: 20 minutes

Ingredients

1 tablespoon Extra Virgin Olive Oil
1 teaspoon Fresh Ginger, minced
1 teaspoon Garlic, minced
1 Jalapeño Pepper, chopped
1 pound Extra Lean Ground Pork
Sea Salt, to taste
Freshly Ground Black Pepper, to taste
4 cups Homemade Vegetable Broth
2 tablespoons Coconut Aminos
1 large Sweet Potato, peeled and spiralized
3-4 Scallions, chopped
4 cups Fresh Spinach, torn

Directions

1. In a large soup pan, heat the oil on a medium heat. Sauté the ginger, garlic and jalapeño pepper for 1 minute. Add the pork and season with salt and black pepper before cooking for 8 to 10 minutes.
2. Add the broth and bring to the boil on a high heat. Reduce the heat, cover and simmer for 8 to 10 minutes. Add the remaining ingredients and, for a further 5 to 6 minutes, simmer before serving.

Lemon Cabbage & Pork

Cabbage makes a perfect accompaniment to ground pork. This dish is absolutely delicious.

MAKES: 4 servings
PREPARATION TIME: 15 minutes
COOKING TIME: 20 minutes

Ingredients

1 tablespoon Fresh Ginger, minced
1 teaspoon Garlic, minced
3 tablespoons Tamari
1 tablespoon Dried Oregano, crushed
1½ tablespoons Extra Virgin Olive Oil
1 Onion, chopped
1 medium Head Cabbage, spiralized
1 pound Extra Lean Ground Pork
3-4 Scallions, chopped
½ cup freshly chopped Parsley Leaves
Sea Salt, to taste
Freshly Ground Black Pepper, to taste
1 tablespoon Fresh Lemon juice

Directions

1. In a bowl, mix together the ginger, garlic, tamari and oregano. Set aside the ginger mixture. In a large skillet, heat 1 tablespoon of oil. Sauté the onion for 4 to 5 minutes. Add the cabbage and half of the ginger mixture. Cook for about 2 to 3 minutes. Transfer the cabbage mixture into a large serving bowl.
2. In the same skillet, heat the remaining oil on a medium heat. Add the pork and remaining ginger mixture. Cook for 8 to 10 minutes. Stir in the scallions, parsley and

seasoning and cook for about 2 minutes. Transfer the pork mixture into the bowl with the cabbage and gently mix together.

3. Drizzle with lemon juice and serve.

Zucchini Roast Pork

This dish is a unique combination of scrumptious zucchini and roasted juicy pork chops, is perfect for special occasions.

MAKES: 2 servings
PREPARATION TIME: 15 minutes
COOKING TIME: 14 minutes

Ingredients

For Pork Chops
2 tablespoons Extra Virgin Olive Oil
2 boneless Pork Chops, trimmed
1 teaspoon Dried Rosemary, crushed
¼ teaspoon Cayenne Pepper
Sea Salt, to taste
Freshly Ground Black Pepper, to taste

For Zucchini
2 large Zucchinis, spiralized
1 cup Fresh Basil Leaves
1 Garlic Clove, minced
½ cup unsalted Cashews, roasted
¼ cup Extra Virgin Olive Oil
¼ cup Organic Coconut Milk
Sea Salt, to taste
Freshly Ground Black Pepper, to taste

Directions

1. For the chops, preheat the oven to 400 degrees F. Heat the oil in a large oven proof skillet on a medium heat. Add the chops and sprinkle with the rosemary and

seasoning. Cook the chops for about 6 minutes, turning once after 3 minutes. Transfer the skillet into the oven and cook for about 8 minutes. Remove the chops from the oven and transfer onto a cutting board. Set aside for 10 minutes. With a sharp knife cut the chops into your desired size pieces.

2. Meanwhile, for the zucchini, place the spiralized zucchini into a large serving bowl. Add all of the remaining ingredients into a food processor and pulse until smooth. Pour the basil mixture over the zucchini and gently toss to coat.

3. Top with the sliced pork and serve.

(16)

FISH & SEAFOOD RECIPES

Zucchini Fish Crunch

This is an absolutely super easy and delicious recipe for dinner. The combination of crunchy zucchini and mahi-mahi makes for a tasty meal.

MAKES: 2 servings
PREPARATION TIME: 15 minutes
COOKING TIME: 12 minutes

Ingredients

2 (4-ounce) Mahi-Mahi Fillets
1 tablespoon Fresh Lemon juice
Sea Salt, to taste
Freshly Ground Black Pepper, to taste
1 Jalapeño Pepper, sliced thinly
2 large Zucchinis, spiralized
¼ cup Organic Coconut Milk
2 tablespoons Extra Virgin Olive Oil

1 Garlic Clove, minced
⅓ cup Fresh Basil Leaves, chopped
2 tablespoons Pumpkin Seeds

Directions

1. Preheat the oven to 400 degrees F and lightly grease a baking dish. Arrange the fish fillets in the prepared baking dish in a single layer and drizzle with the lemon juice. Sprinkle the fillets with salt and black pepper and bake for 6 to 7 minutes. Remove the baking dish from oven. Arrange the jalapeño pepper slices over the fillets and bake for a further 4 to 5 minutes.
2. Place the spiralized zucchini in a large serving bowl. Add the remaining ingredients into a food processor and pulse until smooth. Pour the basil mixture over the zucchini and sprinkle with salt and black pepper before tossing to coat well.
3. Top with the fish fillets and serve.

Herring & Broccoli Pisa

This is a mind blowing and healthy recipe! This delicious dish will keep your dinners exciting, and your diners wanting more.

MAKES: 4 servings
PREPARATION TIME: 20 minutes (plus time to marinate)
COOKING TIME: 20 minutes

Ingredients

For Baked Herring
2 tablespoons Extra Virgin Olive Oil
¼ cup Coconut Aminos
1 tablespoon Fresh Lime juice
2 teaspoons White Sesame Seeds
Sea Salt, to taste
Freshly Ground Black Pepper, to taste
4 (3-ounce) Herring Fillets

For Vegetables
2 large Butternut Squash, peeled and spiralized
2 cups Broccoli Florets
3 tablespoons Extra Virgin Olive Oil
2 teaspoons Fresh Ginger, minced
2 teaspoons Garlic, minced
3 tablespoons Raw Honey
¼ cup Coconut Aminos
2 teaspoons White Sesame Seeds
Sea Salt, to taste
Freshly Ground Black Pepper, to taste
1 teaspoon Black Sesame Seeds

Directions

1. Preheat the oven to 400 degrees F and lightly grease a baking dish.
2. For the fish, in a large bowl mix together all of the ingredients. Refrigerate to marinate for at least 10 minutes. Arrange the fish fillets in the prepared baking dish in a single layer and bake for 10 minutes. Remove the baking dish from oven and place the spiralized squash into the baking dish. Bake for a further 6 to 7 minutes.
3. Meanwhile, for the vegetables, add the broccoli to a pan of boiling water and cook for 6 to 8 minutes. Drain well and set aside. In another pan, heat the oil on a medium heat. Sauté the ginger and garlic for 1 minute before adding the remaining ingredients, except for the white sesame seeds. Stir in the squash and broccoli and cook for 1 to 2 minutes.
4. Place the squash mixture into a serving dish. Top with the fish filets, garnish with the sesame seeds and serve.

Gingery Salmon Delight

This dish makes a delicious combination of healthy ingredients. It is nicely flavored with ginger, garlic and coconut aminos.

MAKES: 2 servings
PREPARATION TIME: 15 minutes
COOKING TIME: 16 minutes

Ingredients

For Grilled Salmon
2 (4-ounce) Salmon Fillets
2 tablespoons Extra Virgin Olive Oil
1 tablespoon Fresh Lime juice
½ teaspoon Garlic Powder
Sea Salt, to taste
Freshly Ground Black Pepper, to taste

For Vegetables
1 tablespoon Extra Virgin Olive Oil
2 teaspoons Fresh Ginger, minced
2 Garlic Cloves, minced
2 cups Fresh Spinach, torn
1½ cups Homemade Vegetable Broth
2 tablespoons Coconut Aminos
3 Zucchinis, spiralized
½ cup Scallions, chopped
Sea Salt, to taste
Freshly Ground Black Pepper, to taste

Directions

1. Preheat the grill to a medium heat and grease the grill

117

grate. Drizzle the salmon fillets with the oil and lime juice and sprinkle with seasoning. Place the fillets under the grill and cook for 6 to 8 minutes per side.

2. Meanwhile, in a skillet heat the oil on a medium heat. Sauté the ginger and garlic for 1 minute. Add the spinach and cook for 1 to 2 minutes. Add the broth and coconut aminos and cook for 2 to 3 minutes. Stir in the spiralized zucchini and cook for 3 to 5 minutes. Stir in scallions and remove the pan from the heat.

3. Place the zucchini mixture onto a serving plate. Top with the salmon and serve.

Potato Salmon Noodles

This is a creative and delicious raw noodle recipe incorporating healthy salmon. This recipe will be a great addition to your menu list.

MAKES: 2 servings
PREPARATION TIME: 15 minutes (plus time to marinate)
COOKING TIME: 45 minutes

Ingredients

For Baked Salmon
2 Garlic Cloves, minced
1 tablespoon Fresh Basil, minced
1 tablespoon Fresh Parsley, minced
¼ cup Extra Virgin Olive Oil
1 tablespoon Fresh Lime juice
Sea Salt, to taste
Freshly Ground Black Pepper, to taste
2 (6-ounce) Salmon Fillets

For Sweet Potato
2 tablespoons Extra Virgin Olive Oil
2 Sweet Potatoes, peeled and spiralized
½ cup Organic Coconut Milk
1 tablespoon Fresh Basil, minced
Sea Salt, to taste
Freshly Ground Black Pepper, to taste

Directions

1. For the fish, in a large bowl mix together all of the ingredients. Refrigerate to marinate for at least 1to 2

hours. Preheat the oven to 375 degrees F and arrange the fish fillets on aluminum foil. Top the fillets with any excess marinade. Fold the foil to seal the fish and place the foil parcels on a baking dish and bake for 35 to 45 minutes.

2. For the sweet potato, in a skillet heat the oil on a medium heat. Add the sweet potato and cook for 1 to 2 minutes. Add the coconut milk, basil, salt and black pepper and cook for 2 to 3 minutes, or until your desired consistency is achieved.

3. Place the sweet potato mixture on a serving plate. Top with the salmon and serve.

Sardine Spiral Salad

This healthy salad has a lovely crunch and absorbs the flavors well. Grilled sardines works nicely with the crunch of the raw vegetables.

MAKES: 4 servings
PREPARATION TIME: 20 minutes (plus time to marinate)
COOKING TIME: 5 minutes

Ingredients

For Grilled Sardines
3 Garlic Cloves, minced
1 teaspoon Dried Thyme, crushed
¼ cup Fresh Lemon juice
¼ cup Extra Virgin Olive Oil
¼ teaspoon Cayenne Pepper
Sea Salt, to taste
Freshly Ground Black Pepper, to taste
1 pound Fresh Sardines, scaled and gutted

For Vegetables
3-4 Zucchinis, spiralized
½ cup Fresh Baby Arugula
2 tablespoons Black Olives, pitted and halved
¼ cup Cherry Tomatoes, halved
1 Garlic Clove, minced
½ teaspoon Lemon Zest, freshly grated
2 tablespoons Fresh Lemon juice
2 tablespoons Extra Virgin Olive Oil
Sea Salt, to taste
Freshly Ground Black Pepper, to taste

121

Directions

1. For the sardines, in a bowl mix together all of the ingredients, except for the sardines. Place the sardines in a large shallow dish in a single layer and coat the sardines with the garlic mixture. Cover and set aside to marinate for at least 1 hour. Preheat the grill to a high heat and grease the grill grate. Place the sardines under the grill and cook for 5 minutes, turning once after 3 minutes. Remove the fish from the grill and let the sardines cool. Now cut into bite size pieces.
2. For the vegetables, in a large serving bowl mix together the spiralized zucchini, arugula, olives and tomatoes. Mix together the remaining ingredients in a separate bowl.
3. Pour the lemon mixture over the vegetables and toss to coat well. Top with the sardine pieces and serve.

Creamy Squash Shrimp

This is an awesome and deliciously creative dinner recipe. Your whole family may love to enjoy this delicious meal time and again.

MAKES: 4 servings
PREPARATION TIME: 15 minutes
COOKING TIME: 12 minutes

Ingredients

2 tablespoons Coconut Oil, Extra Virgin
2 tablespoons Coconut Flour
1½ cups Organic Coconut Milk
⅛ teaspoon chili powder
Sea Salt, to taste
Freshly Ground Black Pepper, to taste
1 teaspoon Dried Thyme, crushed
1 teaspoon Dried Oregano, crushed
1 pound Shrimp, peeled and deveined
1 cup Grape Tomatoes, chopped
1 pound Yellow Squash, spiralized

Directions:

1. In a skillet, heat the oil on a medium heat. Add the coconut flour and, whilst stirring continuously, cook for about 1 minute. Stir in the coconut milk and cook, stirring continuously, for 4 to 5 minutes. Add the seasoning and herbs and cook for a further minute.
2. Stir in the shrimp and tomatoes. Reduce the heat, cover and simmer for 4 to 5 minutes.
3. Place the spiralized squash on a serving plate. Top with the shrimp mixture and serve.

Zoodle Walnut Tuna

This is a wonderful recipe for vegetables with tuna steaks. This recipe will make a super delicious meal every time.

MAKES: 2 servings
PREPARATION TIME: 15 minutes (plus time to marinate)
COOKING TIME: 15 minutes

Ingredients

For Grilled Tuna
1 small Garlic Clove, minced
1 teaspoon Fresh Ginger, minced
1 teaspoon dried Rosemary, crushed
1 tablespoon Extra Virgin Olive Oil
1 tablespoon Coconut Aminos
½ tablespoon Fresh Lime juice
2 (1-inch thick) Tuna Steaks

For Vegetables
4 Garlic Cloves, minced
3 cups freshly chopped Basil Leaves
½ cup and 1 tablespoon Extra Virgin Olive Oil
½ cup Walnuts, chopped
Sea Salt, to taste
Freshly Ground Black Pepper, to taste
½ pound Asparagus, trimmed and cut into 1½-inch pieces
3 Medium Zucchinis, spiralized

Directions

1. For the tuna, in a large bowl mix together all of the ingredients. Cover the bowl with cling film and marinate

for at least 1 hour in the refrigerator. Preheat the grill and place the grill rack 4-inches from the heating element. Grill the fish for 3 minutes per side.

2. For the vegetables, in a food processor add 3 garlic cloves, basil, ½ cup of oil, walnuts, salt and black pepper, and pulse until smooth before setting aside. In a skillet, heat the remaining oil on a medium heat. Add the remaining garlic and sauté for 1 minute. Add the asparagus and cook for 4 to 5 minutes. Meanwhile, in a pan of boiling water add the spiralized zucchini and cook for 2 to 3 minutes. Drain well and pat dry with a paper towel.

3. On a serving plate mix together the zucchini, asparagus and basil mixture. Top with the grilled tuna and serve.

Shrimp Veggie Pasta

In this recipe the almond butter sauce compliments nicely with the zucchini, asparagus and shrimp. A garnishing of sesame seeds and scallions adds a nice twist to this dish.

MAKES: 4 servings
PREPARATION TIME: 20 minutes
COOKING TIME: 13 minutes

Ingredients

1 cup Asparagus, trimmed and cut into 1½-inch pieces
4 medium Yellow Squash, spiralized
1½ pounds large Shrimp, peeled and deveined
¼ teaspoon Fresh Ginger, minced
½ teaspoon Garlic, minced
½ cup Coconut Aminos
½ cup Almond Butter
Sea Salt, to taste
Freshly Ground Black Pepper, to taste
¼ cup Scallions, sliced thinly
1 tablespoon White Sesame Seeds

Directions

1. Arrange a steamer basket over a pan of boiling water. Place the asparagus in the steamer basket. Cover and steam for 4 to 5 minutes, or until done. Transfer the asparagus into a colander. Place the spiralized squash in the steamer basket and steam for about 3 minutes. Transfer the squash into the colander and set aside to drain completely. Place the shrimp in the same steamer basket and steam for 4 to 5 minutes. Transfer the

shrimp, squash and asparagus onto a serving plate.

2. Meanwhile, in a bowl, mix together the ginger, garlic, coconut aminos and almond butter. Season with salt and pepper if required. Pour the almond butter sauce over the shrimp and zucchini, gently tossing to thoroughly mix the dish.

3. Top with the scallions and sesame seeds and serve.

Shrimp & Tomato Zoodles

Zucchini noodles with shrimp, cherry tomatoes and fresh lime juice makes a really delicious dish. Enjoy every bite.

MAKES: 2 servings
PREPARATION TIME: 15 minutes
COOKING TIME: 8 minutes

Ingredients

1 tablespoon Coconut Oil, Extra Virgin
3 Garlic Cloves, minced
½ pound Shrimp, peeled and deveined
2 large Zucchinis, spiralized
⅛ teaspoon chili powder
Sea Salt, to taste
Freshly Ground Black Pepper, to taste
½ cup Cherry Tomatoes, halved
1 tablespoon Fresh Lime juice

Directions

1. In a large skillet, heat ½ tablespoon of oil on a medium-high heat. Add 2 garlic cloves and sauté for 30 seconds. Add the shrimp and sprinkle with seasoning. Cook for 3 to 4 minutes. Transfer the shrimp onto a plate and set aside.
2. In the same skillet, heat the remaining oil on a medium heat. Add the remaining garlic and sauté for 30 seconds. Add the zucchini and cook for 1 to 2 minutes. Stir in the tomatoes, shrimp and lime juice and cook for 1 minute.
3. Remove from the heat and serve immediately.

Garlic Shrimp Spirals

This classic recipe combines sweet potato noodles with olives,
capers and shrimp very nicely. A great dinner recipe indeed!

MAKES: 4 servings
PREPARATION TIME: 20 minutes
COOKING TIME: 18 minutes

Ingredients

1 tablespoon Coconut Oil, Extra Virgin
3 Garlic Cloves, minced
3 cups Fresh Tomatoes, finely chopped
¼ cup Homemade Vegetable Broth
¼ cup Green Olives, pitted and halved
¼ cup Capers
¼ cup Fresh Cilantro, chopped
¼ teaspoon Cayenne Pepper
Sea Salt, to taste
Freshly Ground Black Pepper, to taste
2 large Sweet Potatoes, peeled and spiralized
14-16 medium Shrimp, peeled and deveined

Directions

1. In a large skillet, heat the oil on a medium-low heat. Sauté the garlic for 1 minute. Add the tomatoes and cook for 1 to 2 minutes, crushing them. Add the broth, olives, capers, 2 tablespoons of cilantro, cayenne pepper, salt and black pepper. Cook, stirring occasionally, for 4 to 5 minutes.
2. Stir in the spiralized sweet potatoes. Cover and cook for 4 to 5 minutes, tossing once after 2 minutes. Gently stir

in the shrimp. Cover and cook for a further 5 minutes.
3. Garnish with the remaining cilantro and serve.

Zucchini Scallops Combo

This mouthwatering recipe is quick and easy to prepare and is delicious in every way. Enjoy this zucchini scallop dish any time you want.

MAKES: 4 servings
PREPARATION TIME: 15 minutes
COOKING TIME: 10 minutes

Ingredients

3 tablespoons Extra Virgin Olive Oil
2 Garlic Cloves, minced
6-7 medium Zucchinis, spiralized
Sea Salt, to taste
Freshly Ground Black Pepper, to taste
1 tablespoon Fresh Lemon Juice
4 Scallions, chopped (white and green parts separated)
1 pound Bay Scallops, cleaned, rinsed and pat dried

Directions

1. In a large skillet, heat 2 tablespoons of the oil on a medium-high heat. Sauté the garlic for 1 minute. Add the spiralized zucchini and sprinkle with salt and black pepper. Cook for 4 to 5 minutes. Transfer the zucchini onto a plate. Drizzle with the lime juice and stir in the white part of the scallions.
2. In the same skillet, heat the remaining oil on a medium-high heat. Add the scallops and cook for about 4 minutes, tossing once after 2 minutes. Transfer the scallops onto the plate with the zucchini.
3. Top the dish with the green parts of the scallions and

serve.

Parsnip Carrot Pleasure

This is a simple and yet nutritious and delicious parsnip noodle recipe. This dish is flavor packed and is a great way to get extra nutrients into your diet.

MAKES: 4 servings
PREPARATION TIME: 15 minutes
COOKING TIME: 15 minutes

Ingredients

3 tablespoons Extra Virgin Olive Oil
2 large Carrots, peeled and sliced thinly
1 large Onion, sliced thinly
1 Garlic Clove, minced
1 pound Parsnips, peeled and spiralized
2 tablespoons Coconut Aminos
Sea Salt, to taste
Freshly Ground Black Pepper, to taste
1 pound Shrimps, peeled and deveined
2 tablespoons White Sesame Seeds

Directions

1. In a large skillet, heat the oil on a medium heat. Add the carrots and onion and sauté for 3 to 4 minutes before sautéing the garlic for 1 minute. Add the spiralized parsnip and sauté for 6 to 7 minutes. Stir in the coconut aminos, salt and black pepper.
2. Meanwhile, arrange a steamer basket over a pan of boiling water. Place the shrimp into the steamer basket and steam for 4 to 5 minutes. Transfer the shrimp into the skillet and cook for 2 to3 minutes.

3. Top with the sesame seeds and serve.

Zucchini Lobster Bowl

The combination of lobster with vegetables makes for a perfect and tasty dish for summertime celebrations.

MAKES: 2 servings
PREPARATION TIME: 15 minutes
COOKING TIME: 30 minutes

Ingredients

2 tablespoons Coconut Oil, Extra Virgin
2 (4-ounce) Lobster Tails, shelled and cut into bite size pieces
½ small Onion, chopped
2 Garlic Cloves, minced
2 cups Fresh Tomatoes, finely chopped
½ cup Homemade Vegetable Broth
¼ teaspoon Chili Powder
Sea Salt, to taste
Freshly Ground Black Pepper, to taste
2-3 medium Zucchinis, spiralized
1 tablespoon minced Cilantro

Directions

1. In a large skillet, heat 1 tablespoon of oil on a medium heat. Add the lobster tails and cook for 6 to 7 minutes. Transfer the lobster onto a serving plate.
2. In the same skillet, heat the remaining oil on a medium heat. Sauté the onion for 4 to 5 minutes before sautéing the garlic for 1 minute. Add the tomatoes and cook for 3 to 4 minutes, crushing them. Add the broth and seasoning, and bring the pan to the boil. Reduce the heat

135

and simmer for 10 to 15 minutes. Stir in the zucchini and lobster meat and cook for an additional 5 minutes.

3. Garnish with cilantro and serve.

Sweet Potato Clams

This very simple recipe has a nice depth of flavor with the addition of the broth. This dish will be liked by all!

MAKES: 2 servings
PREPARATION TIME: 15 minutes
COOKING TIME: 12 minutes

Ingredients

1 tablespoon Extra Virgin Olive Oil
1 small White Onion, chopped
1 Celery Stalk, chopped
2 small Garlic Cloves, minced
¼ cup Homemade Fish Broth
1 tablespoon Fresh Lime juice
10 little Neck Clams
3 teaspoons Fresh Thyme, chopped
¼ teaspoon Chili Powder
Sea Salt, to taste
Freshly Ground Black Pepper, to taste
1 large Sweet Potato, peeled and spiralized

Directions

1. In a skillet, heat the oil on a medium heat. Sauté the onion and celery for 3 to 4 minutes before sautéing the garlic for 1 minute. Add the broth and lime juice and bring to the boil. Add the clams and reduce the heat to medium-low. Cover and simmer for 6 to 7 minutes. Stir in the thyme and seasoning and immediately remove the pan from the heat.
2. Meanwhile, place the spiralized sweet potato into a

steamer basket. Arrange the basket over a pan of boiling water and steam for 6 to 8 minutes, until tender. Transfer the sweet potato into a serving bowl. Top with clam mixture and serve.

Zucchini Pasta Mussels

This gourmet meal is really simple to prepare. This incredibly flavorful and fulfilling dish will always be a perfect hit for dinner.

MAKES: 4 servings
PREPARATION TIME: 20 minutes
COOKING TIME: 12 minutes

Ingredients

1 tablespoon Coconut Oil, Extra Virgin
1 cup Yellow Onion, chopped
2 Celery Stalks, chopped
2 Garlic Cloves, minced
2 cups Grape Tomatoes, halved
¼ teaspoon Cayenne Pepper
Sea Salt, to taste
Freshly Ground Black Pepper, to taste
20-24 Mussels, scrubbed and de-bearded
2 tablespoons Fresh Parsley, chopped
4 zucchinis, spiralized

Directions

1. In a skillet, heat the oil on a medium heat. Sauté the onion and celery for 3 to 4 minutes before sautéing the garlic for 1 minute. Stir in the tomatoes and seasoning. Cover and cook for 4 to 5 minutes.
2. Reduce the heat to low and stir in the mussels and parsley. Cover and cook for about 2 minutes.
3. Place the spiralized zucchini into a large serving bowl. Add the mussel mixture and gently toss to coat before serving.

POULTRY RECIPES

Zucchini Chicken Soup

This is a delicate and delicious soup recipe for the whole family. The use of fresh lemon juice and herbs adds a wonderful touch to this dish.

MAKES: 2 servings
PREPARATION TIME: 15 minutes
COOKING TIME: 32 minutes

Ingredients

1 tablespoon Extra Virgin Olive Oil
⅓ cup Onion, chopped
1 Stalk Celery, chopped
2 teaspoons Garlic, minced
½ Jalapeño Pepper, seeded and chopped
1 teaspoon Chili Powder
1¾ cups Tomatoes, chopped finely
1 teaspoon Dried Thyme, crushed
1 tablespoon Fresh Lemon juice
3 cups Homemade Chicken Broth

Sea Salt, to taste
Freshly Ground Black Pepper, to taste
2 medium Zucchinis, spiralized
1 Avocado, peeled, pitted and cubed
1 Grass-Fed cooked skinless, boneless shredded cooked
Chicken Breast
1 tablespoon Fresh Parsley, chopped

Directions

1. In a large soup pan, heat the oil on a medium heat. Add the onion and celery and sauté for 4 to 5 minutes. Add the garlic and sauté for 1 minute more. Add the jalapeño and chili powder, and sauté for a further minute. Add the tomatoes and thyme and cook for 3 to 4 minutes.
2. Add the lemon juice, broth, black pepper and salt. Bring the dish to the boil before reducing the heat. Cover and simmer for 15 to 20 minutes. Stir in spiralized zucchini, avocado, chicken and parsley, and cook for 2 minutes more.
3. Remove from the heat and serve hot.

Cucumber Chicken Salad

This light and refreshing salad is a great option for light lunch. This dish is also a fun salad to make.

MAKES: 4 servings
PREPARATION TIME: 20 minutes

Ingredients

3 large Cucumbers, spiralized and pat dried
1 Avocado, peeled, pitted and cubed
10-12 Black Olives, pitted and halved
2 Grass-Fed cooked skinless, boneless, Chicken Breasts (cubed)
2 tablespoons Extra Virgin Olive Oil
2 tablespoons Fresh Lemon juice
1 small Red Onion, chopped
1 Garlic Clove, minced
3 tablespoons diced Parsley Leaves
Sea Salt, to taste
Freshly Ground Black Pepper, to taste
½ cup Pecans, chopped

Directions

1. In a large serving bowl, mix together the spiralized cucumber, avocado, olives and chicken.
2. In a food processor, add all of the remaining ingredients, except for the pecans, and pulse until pureed. Pour the dressing over the cucumber mixture and gently toss to coat.
3. Top with the pecans and serve.

Sautéed Chicken Zoodles

This is a super quick and delicious dinner idea. This dish may be a perfect hit for summer when it is too hot to spend too long in the kitchen.

MAKES: 4 servings
PREPARATION TIME: 15 minutes
COOKING TIME: 8 minutes

Ingredients

1½ tablespoons Olive Oil, Extra Virgin
1 Garlic Clove, minced
1 pound Grass-Fed skinless, boneless Chicken Breast
Sea Salt, to taste
Freshly Ground Black Pepper, to taste
3 large Zucchinis, spiralized
1 Jalapeño Pepper, chopped
1 tablespoon Fresh Lemon Juice
½ cup Fresh Parsley, chopped

Directions

1. In a large skillet, heat ½ tablespoons of oil on a medium-high heat. Sauté the garlic for 30 seconds. Dice the chicken breast and sauté for 4 to 5 minutes. Stir in the salt and black pepper, and sauté for 30 seconds more. Transfer the chicken into a bowl.
2. In the same skillet, heat the remaining oil on medium-high heat. Add the spiralized zucchini and sauté for 1 to 2 minutes. Stir in the chicken, jalapeño, lemon juice and parsley, and remove from the heat.
3. Serve hot.

143

Veggie Medley Chicken Soup

This is an awesome idea for a delicious and healthy soup. This recipe is also a creative way to get your little ones to eat vegetables!

MAKES: 4 servings
PREPARATION TIME: 15 minutes
COOKING TIME: 38 minutes

Ingredients

2 tablespoons Extra Virgin Olive Oil
1 medium White Onion, chopped
3 Garlic Cloves, minced
2 cups Celery, chopped
3 cups Carrots, peeled and chopped
7-8 cups Homemade Chicken Broth
3 large Zucchinis, spiralized
2 Grass-Fed cooked, skinless, boneless, shredded Chicken Breasts
Sea Salt, to taste
Freshly Ground Black Pepper, to taste

Directions

1. In a large soup pan, heat the oil on a medium heat. Sauté the onion for 4 to 5 minutes before sautéing the garlic for 1 minute. Add the celery and carrots and cook for 3 to 4 minutes.
2. Add the broth and bring the pan to the boil. Reduce the heat, cover and simmer for 20 to 25 minutes. Stir in the spiralized zucchini and chicken, and cook for 2 to 3 minutes more.

3. Season with salt and pepper, remove from the heat and
    serve hot.

Sautéed Sqoodle Chicken

This is a satisfying and flavorful meal for lunch or dinner. This dish will keep you satisfied and fueled all day!

MAKES: 2 servings
PREPARATION TIME: 10 minutes
COOKING TIME: 15 minutes

Ingredients

*1½ tablespoons Extra Virgin Olive Oil
1 Garlic Clove, minced
2 (6-ounce) Grass-Fed boneless, skinless Chicken Breasts, cubed
Sea Salt, to taste
Freshly Ground Black Pepper, to taste
2 cups Fresh Kale, trimmed and chopped
2 large Yellow Squash, spiralized
1 tablespoon Fresh Lime juice*

Directions

1. In a large skillet, heat the oil on a medium heat. Sauté the garlic for 1 minute. Add the chicken and season with salt and black pepper. Cook for 6 to 8 minutes until golden brown.
2. Add the kale and cook for a further 2 to 3 minutes. Stir in the spiralized squash and lime juice. Cook for another 2 to 3 minutes before serving hot.

Chicken Broccoli Zoodles

This recipe, which nicely combines zucchini and broccoli with chicken, creates a rich yet simple dish.

MAKES: 2 servings
PREPARATION TIME: 10 minutes
COOKING TIME: 18 minutes

Ingredients

2 tablespoons Extra Virgin Olive Oil
1 large Garlic Clove, minced
2 (6-ounce) Grass-Fed boneless, skinless Chicken Breasts, cubed
¼ teaspoon Red Chili Powder
Sea Salt, to taste
Freshly Ground Black Pepper, to taste
1 Broccoli Head, cut into florets
¾ cup Homemade Chicken Broth
2 large Zucchinis, spiralized
1 tablespoon Fresh Oregano, chopped

Directions

1. In a large skillet, heat the oil on a medium heat. Sauté the garlic for 1 minute. Add the chicken and sprinkle with the chili powder, salt and black pepper. Cook for 6 to 8 minutes, or until golden brown on all sides.
2. Add the broccoli and cook for 2 to 3 minutes. Add the broth and cook for a further 2 to 3 minutes. Stir in the zucchini and oregano, and cook for 2 to 3 minutes more.
3. Serve hot.

Swoodle Chicken & Asparagus

The combination of sweet potato, chicken, asparagus and lemon juice makes a wonderfully delicious meal for the whole family.

MAKES: 2 servings
PREPARATION TIME: 15 minutes
COOKING TIME: 17 minutes

Ingredients

2 tablespoons Extra Virgin Olive Oil
1 large Garlic Clove, minced
2 (4-ounce) Grass-Fed boneless, skinless Chicken Breasts,
cubed
Sea Salt, to taste
Freshly Ground Black Pepper, to taste
1 large Sweet Potato, peeled and spiralized
½ cup Homemade Chicken Broth
6-8 Asparagus Stalks, shaved and trimmed
2 tablespoons Fresh Basil, chopped
½ tablespoon Fresh Lemon juice

Directions

1. In a large skillet, heat the oil on a medium heat. Sauté the garlic for 1 minute. Add the chicken and sprinkle with salt and black pepper. Cook for 6 to 8 minutes, or until golden brown on all sides.
2. Add the spiralized sweet potato and broth, and cook for 2 to 3 minutes. Stir in the asparagus and basil, and cook for a further 4 to 5 minutes.
3. Drizzle with lemon juice and serve hot.

Zucchini Kale Chicken

This is a healthy and flavorful dish with lemon adding a refreshingly zesty taste.

MAKES: 2 servings
PREPARATION TIME: 15 minutes
COOKING TIME: 27 minutes

Ingredients

2 (4-ounce) Grass-Fed boneless, skinless Chicken Breasts, sliced into thin strips
1½ tablespoons Fresh Lemon juice
2 teaspoons Dried Rosemary, crushed
½ teaspoon Cayenne pepper
Sea Salt, to taste
Freshly Ground Black Pepper, to taste
1 tablespoon Extra Virgin Olive Oil
1 Garlic Clove, minced
2 cups Fresh Kale, trimmed and chopped
2 large Zucchinis, spiralized
1 teaspoon Lemon Zest, freshly grated

Directions

1. Preheat the oven to 350 degrees F and grease a baking dish. Place the chicken strips into the prepared baking dish. Drizzle with 1 tablespoon of lemon juice. Sprinkle with rosemary, ¼ teaspoon of cayenne pepper, salt and black pepper. Bake for 15 to 20 minutes before removing from the oven and setting aside.
2. Meanwhile, in a large skillet, heat the oil on a medium heat. Sauté the garlic for 1 minute. Add the kale and cook

149

for about 3 minutes. Stir in the spiralized zucchini, remaining cayenne pepper and lemon juice. Cook whilst stirring occasionally for 2 to 3 minutes before adding the chicken.

3. Remove from the heat, garnish with lemon zest and serve hot.

Baked Squash Chicken

Make this tasty and flavorful dish for your family and friends and you will receive loads of appreciation.

MAKES: 4 servings
PREPARATION TIME: 15 minutes
COOKING TIME: 45 minutes

Ingredients

4-6 medium Yellow Squash, spiralized
3 tablespoons Extra Virgin Olive Oil
Sea Salt, to taste
Freshly Ground Black Pepper, to taste
1 pound skinless, boneless Chicken Breast strips
1 White Onion, chopped
3-4 Garlic Cloves, minced
¾ pound Grape Tomatoes, halved
1¼ cups Homemade Chicken Broth
½ cup Fresh Baby Spinach
1 tablespoon Fresh Oregano
1 tablespoon Fresh Thyme, chopped

Directions

1. Preheat the oven to 400 degrees F and grease a baking sheet. Place the spiralized squash onto the prepared baking sheet. Drizzle with 1 tablespoon of oil and sprinkle with salt and black pepper. Bake for about 10 minutes. Remove from the oven and toss the squash. Bake for 15 minutes more before removing from the oven and setting aside.
2. In a large skillet, heat 1 tablespoon of oil on a medium

151

heat. Add the chicken and sprinkle with salt and black pepper. Cook for 8 to 10 minutes, or until golden brown on all sides. Transfer the chicken onto a plate.

3. In the same skillet, heat the remaining oil on a medium heat. Add the onion and sauté for 3 to 4 minutes before adding the garlic and sautéing for 1 minute more. Add the tomatoes and broth, and cook for 2 to 3 minutes. Add the chicken, squash, spinach and herbs and cook for a further 2 minutes before serving hot.

Coconut Chicken Pumpkin

This is a great vegetable noodle with chicken recipe, ideal for the fall months. The pumpkin puree in this dish adds a classic twist to this chicken and squash meal.

MAKES: 4 servings
PREPARATION TIME: 15 minutes
COOKING TIME: 20 minutes

Ingredients

2 tablespoons Extra Virgin Olive Oil
1 small White Onion, chopped
2 Garlic Cloves, minced
2 cups Homemade Pumpkin Puree
½ cup Organic Coconut Milk
2 cups Homemade Chicken Broth
2 tablespoons minced Basil Leaves
Sea Salt, to taste
Freshly Ground Black Pepper, to taste
4 large Yellow Squash, spiralized
1 pound Grilled Grass-Fed skinless, boneless, cubed Chicken Breast

Directions

1. In a large skillet, heat the oil on a medium-low heat. Sauté the onion for 3 to 4 minutes before sautéing the garlic for 1 minute. Stir in the pumpkin puree, coconut milk, broth, 1 tablespoon of basil and seasoning. Reduce the heat to low, simmer and stir occasionally for about 10 minutes.
2. Stir in the spiralized squash and chicken, and cook for 4

153

to 5 minutes.
3. Top with the remaining basil and serve hot.

Creamy Chicken Swoodle

This is an inspiringly delicious recipe! The creamy sauce in this dish combines beautifully with the sweet potato, chicken and scallions.

MAKES: 4 servings
PREPARATION TIME: 20 minutes
COOKING TIME: 27 minutes

Ingredients

For Creamy Sauce
4½ cups Cauliflower, chopped
1 small Garlic Clove, minced
1½ cups Organic Coconut Milk
½ cup Homemade Chicken Broth
Sea Salt, to taste

For Scallions
1 tablespoon Extra Virgin Olive Oil
4 cups Scallions, sliced
1 tablespoon Fresh Lime juice
2 tablespoons Homemade Chicken Broth

For Assembling
2 large Sweet Potatoes, peeled and spiralized
2 cups Grilled Grass-Fed skinless, boneless, cubed Chicken Breast
Sea Salt, to taste
Freshly Ground Black Pepper, to taste
1 teaspoon Lime Zest, freshly grated
3 tablespoons minced Cilantro Leaves

Directions

1. For the sauce, in a pan of boiling water add the cauliflower and cook for about 10 minutes. Drain well and cool slightly. In a blender, add the cauliflower and remaining sauce ingredients, and pulse until creamy and smooth. Transfer into a large bowl and set aside.
2. In a large skillet, heat the oil on a low heat. Add the scallions and cook for about 15 minutes. Stir in the lime juice, broth and salt, and cook for 5 minutes more. Remove from the heat and add to the bowl with the creamy sauce.
3. In another pan of boiling water, add the spiralized sweet potato and cook for about 4 to 5 minutes. Drain well. In a large skillet, add the scallion mixture, sweet potato and chicken and cook for 2 minutes, or until it is warm. Season with salt and black pepper. Top with lime zest and cilantro and serve immediately.

Parsnip Herbed Chicken

This is a great vegetable noodle and chicken dish for dinner. The herbs used in this recipe add a classic touch to this delicious dish.

MAKES: 2 servings
PREPARATION TIME: 15 minutes
COOKING TIME: 15 minutes

Ingredients

For Grilled Chicken
¼ cup Extra Virgin Olive Oil
2 Garlic Cloves, minced
1 teaspoon Dried Rosemary, crushed
Sea Salt, to taste
Freshly Ground Black Pepper, to taste
2 Grass-Fed skinless, boneless Chicken Breast Halves

For Vegetables
½ cup Homemade Chicken Broth
2 large Carrots, peeled and spiralized
2 large Parsnips, peeled and spiralized
1 teaspoon Dried Rosemary, crushed
1 teaspoon Dried Thyme, crushed
1 teaspoon Dried Oregano, crushed
Sea Salt, to taste
Freshly Ground Black Pepper, to taste
2 tablespoons Fresh Parsley, chopped

Directions

1. Preheat the grill. Mix together all of the chicken ingredients in a large bowl, except for the chicken. Add

the chicken and coat with the mixture. Grill the chicken breasts for 15 minutes, turning frequently. Remove the chicken from the oven and transfer onto a cutting board. Set aside for 10 minutes. With a sharp knife cut into your desired size pieces.

2. Meanwhile, in a large skillet on a medium heat, add the broth and remaining vegetable ingredients, except for the fresh parsley. Cook, stirring occasionally, for 4 to 5 minutes or until cooked.

3. Top with the broiled chicken, garnish with parsley and serve.

Chicken Zoodles Roast

This will be a hit recipe for the whole family. These zucchini noodles with chicken and roasted tomatoes are the perfect way to enjoy fresh vegetables.

MAKES: 2 servings
PREPARATION TIME: 15 minutes
COOKING TIME: 23 minutes

Ingredients

2 cups Grape Tomatoes
1 tablespoon Extra Virgin Olive Oil
Sea Salt, to taste
Freshly Ground Black Pepper, to taste
2 Garlic Cloves, minced
2 cups Mixed Fresh Greens (Kale, Spinach, Arugula), torn
2 large Zucchinis, spiralized
1 cup cooked Grass-Fed skinless, boneless, cubed Chicken Breast

Directions

1. Preheat the oven to 400 degrees F and arrange the grape tomatoes in a baking dish. Evenly drizzle with oil and sprinkle with salt and black pepper. Roast for about 20 minutes. Remove from oven and set aside.
2. Meanwhile, in a large skillet heat the oil on a medium heat. Sauté the garlic for 1 minute. Add the greens and cook for 2 to 3 minutes. Add the spiralized zucchini, cooked chicken and roasted tomatoes and cook, whilst stirring occasionally, for 2 to 3 minutes.
3. Serve hot.

159

Parsnip Chicken Capers

This is a wonderfully delicious way to use parsnip. The baked chicken in this recipe makes a perfect combination with the spiralized parsnip.

MAKES: 2 servings
PREPARATION TIME: 15 minutes
COOKING TIME: 25 minutes

Ingredients

For Baked Chicken
2 Grass-Fed skinless, boneless Chicken Thighs
1 tablespoon Extra Virgin Olive Oil
½ teaspoon Cayenne Pepper
Sea Salt, to taste
Freshly Ground Black Pepper, to taste

For Parsnip
1 tablespoon Extra Virgin Olive Oil
1 Garlic Clove, minced
6 Parsnips, peeled and spiralized
1 tablespoon Capers
2 tablespoons minced Cilantro Leaves

Directions

1. Preheat the oven to 425 degrees F and lightly grease a baking pan. Arrange the chicken thighs in the prepared baking dish. Drizzle with oil and sprinkle with spices. Bake for 20 to 25 minutes. Remove the thighs from oven and transfer onto a cutting board. Set aside for 10 minutes. With a sharp knife cut your desired size pieces.

2. Meanwhile, in a large skillet, heat the oil on a medium heat. Sauté the garlic for 1 minute. Stir in the spiralized parsnip and reduce the heat to low. Cover and cook, whilst stirring occasionally, for 15 to 20 minutes. Stir in the capers and cilantro and immediately remove from the heat.
3. Top with the chicken and serve.

Pecan Chicken Spaghetti

This vegetable noodle and chicken dish is dressed with spinach, basil and pecans sauce. This is a flavorful and rich dish ideal for lunch.

MAKES: 2 servings
PREPARATION TIME: 20 minutes

Ingredients

5 Radishes, spiralized
1 large Zucchini, spiralized
2 cups Fresh Baby Spinach
½ cup Fresh Basil, chopped
1 Garlic Clove, minced
¾ cup Pecans, chopped and divided
1 tablespoon Fresh Lemon juice
½ Cup Water
Sea Salt, to taste
Freshly Ground Black Pepper, to taste
1 cup Grilled Grass-Fed skinless, boneless, cubed Chicken Thighs

Directions

1. Place the spiralized radishes and zucchini into a large serving bowl.
2. In a food processor, add the spinach, basil, garlic, ½ cup of pecans, lemon juice, water, salt and black pepper, and pulse until smooth. Pour the spinach mixture over the vegetables and gently toss to coat.
3. Top with the grilled chicken, garnish with remaining pecans and serve.

Sweet Potato Arugula Turkey

This is a beautifully colored and tasty dish for a family dinner. The cooked turkey combines perfectly with the sweet potatoes and arugula.

MAKES: 2 servings
PREPARATION TIME: 15 minutes
COOKING TIME: 13 minutes

Ingredients

1 tablespoon Extra Virgin Olive Oil
½ cup Yellow Onion, chopped
1 large Garlic Clove, minced
1 large Sweet Potato, peeled and spiralized
Sea Salt, to taste
Freshly Ground Black Pepper, to taste
1 cup cooked, diced, skinless, boneless Turkey Breast
¼ cup Homemade Chicken Broth
3 cups Arugula, chopped
1 tablespoon Fresh Basil, chopped

Directions

1. In a large skillet, heat the oil on a medium heat. Sauté the onion and garlic for 3 to 4 minutes.
2. Add the spiralized sweet potato and sprinkle with salt and black pepper. Cook for 2 to 3 minutes. Add the cooked turkey and broth, and cook for a further 2 to 3 minutes. Add the arugula and basil, and cook for 3 minutes more.
3. Serve hot.

Zucchini with Turkey Meatballs

This is a great combination of meatballs with vegetable noodles.
The ingredients in this dish will delight your taste buds!

MAKES: 2 servings
PREPARATION TIME: 15 minutes
COOKING TIME: 15 minutes

Ingredients

For Meatballs
½ pound Lean Ground Turkey
1½ tablespoons Coconut Milk
1 tablespoon Coconut Flour
¼ teaspoon Dried Oregano, crushed
¼ teaspoon Dried Thyme, crushed
Sea Salt, to taste
Freshly Ground Black Pepper, to taste

For Zucchini
2 large Zucchinis, spiralized
3 cups Fresh Spinach, chopped
1 Garlic Clove, minced
3 tablespoons Walnuts, chopped
2 tablespoons Almond Butter
3 tablespoons Extra Virgin Olive Oil
1½ tablespoons Fresh Lemon juice
3 tablespoons Water
Sea Salt, to taste
Freshly Ground Black Pepper, to taste

Directions

1. Preheat the oven to 400 degrees F and line a baking sheet with parchment paper. For the meatballs, in a large bowl combine together all of the ingredients. Make your desired size balls from the mixture. Arrange the meatballs on the prepared baking sheet in a single layer. Bake for 12 to 15 minutes, or until cooked.
2. Meanwhile, in a large serving bowl place the spiralized zucchini. In a food processor, add all of the remaining ingredients and pulse until smooth. Pour the spinach mixture over the zucchini and gently toss to coat.
3. Top with the meatballs and serve.

Tomato Squash Turkey

This is a classic and lighter dish for an enjoyable dinner. This dish combines the rich and meaty flavors of ground turkey with spiralized squash.

MAKES: 2 servings
PREPARATION TIME: 15 minutes
COOKING TIME: 40 minutes

Ingredients

2 tablespoons Extra Virgin Olive Oil
½ pound Lean Ground Turkey
1 teaspoon Dried Thyme, crushed
½ cup White Onion, chopped
2 Garlic Cloves, minced
¾ cup Carrots, peeled and chopped finely
½ cup Celery, chopped finely
1 cup Tomatoes, crushed
½ cup Homemade Chicken Broth
3 tablespoons Fresh Oregano, chopped
Sea Salt, to taste
Freshly Ground Black Pepper, to taste
2 large Yellow Squash, spiralized

Directions

1. In a large skillet, heat 1 tablespoon of oil on a medium heat. Add the turkey and thyme and cook for 4 to 5 minutes, or until golden brown. Transfer the turkey into a bowl.
2. In the same skillet, heat the remaining oil on a medium heat. Add the onion and sauté for 3 to 4 minutes before

sautéing the garlic for 1 minute. Sauté the carrot and celery for 2 to 3 minutes. Add the tomatoes and turkey and cook, stirring occasionally, for 4 to 5 minutes.

3. Add the broth, oregano and seasoning and bring to the boil. Reduce the heat and, for 15 to 20 minutes, simmer until the sauce thickens. Stir in the squash and cook for a further 2 minutes. Serve hot.

Sweet Turkey Cranberries

This delicious dish is packed with all insanely comforting flavors. Cranberries bring a wonderful flavor to this savory dish.

MAKES: 2 servings
PREPARATION TIME: 15 minutes
COOKING TIME: 15 minutes

Ingredients

1 tablespoon Extra Virgin Olive Oil
1 White onion, chopped
1 Garlic Clove, minced
1 large Sweet Potato, peeled and spiralized
¼ cup Fresh Cranberries
1 tablespoon Fresh Parsley, chopped
½ tablespoon Ground Cinnamon
Sea Salt, to taste
Freshly Ground Black Pepper, to taste
1 cup grilled, diced, boneless Turkey Breast

Directions

1. In a large skillet, heat the oil on a medium heat. Sauté the onion for 3 to 4 minutes before sautéing the garlic for 1 minute. Add all of the remaining ingredients, except for the turkey, and cook for 6 to 8 minutes.
2. Stir in the grilled turkey and cook for 2 minutes more before serving hot.

Roasted Duck Zoodles

Spiralized zucchini comes out very nicely with roasted duck. Your toddlers will love to eat this delicious dish.

MAKES: 2 servings
PREPARATION TIME: 15 minutes
COOKING TIME: 2 hours

Ingredients

For Roasted Duck
1 (5-pound) Grass-Fed Whole Duck
1 teaspoon Cayenne Pepper
Sea Salt, to taste
Freshly Ground Black Pepper, to taste
½ cup melted Coconut Oil, Extra Virgin

For Zucchini
3-4 large Zucchinis, spiralized
1½ cups Grape Tomatoes, halved
1 tablespoon Extra Virgin Olive Oil
1 Garlic Clove, minced
1 cup Fresh Basil Leaves, chopped
Sea Salt, to taste
Freshly Ground Black Pepper, to taste

Directions

1. Preheat the oven to 375 degrees F and line a roasting pan with parchment paper. Arrange the duck in the prepared roasting pan. Generously rub the duck with the spices and roast for about 1 hour. Pour half of the melted oil over the duck and roast for a further 45 minutes. Pour

the remaining oil over the duck and roast for 15 minutes more. Remove the duck from the oven and transfer onto a cutting board. Set aside for 15 minutes. With a sharp knife cut into your desired size pieces.

2. Meanwhile, in a large serving bowl place the spiralized zucchini and remaining ingredients, and mix. Top with sliced duck and serve immediately.

HOLIDAY RECIPES

Sweet & Sour Vegetable Salad

This is a wonderfully delicious salad for the whole family. The use of lemon juice in this recipe adds a refreshing touch in this dish.

MAKES: 2 servings
PREPARATION TIME: 20 minutes

Ingredients

1 medium Cucumber, spiralized
1 medium Zucchini, spiralized
½ cup Red Onion, chopped
3 tablespoons Fresh Lemon juice
1 teaspoon Organic Honey
Sea Salt, to taste
Freshly Ground Black Pepper, to taste
1 tablespoon Sesame Seeds

Directions

1. In a large bowl, mix together the spiralized cucumber, zucchini and onion. Mix together all of the remaining ingredients in a separate bowl before mixing the dressing with the salad.
2. Cover and refrigerate to chill completely. Top with sesame seeds before serving.

Apple Strawberries Greens

This recipe makes a really delicious salad with the combination of fresh greens with spiralized apple and strawberries. The sweet and sour dressing adds a delicious touch.

MAKES: 2 servings
PREPARATION TIME: 20 minutes

Ingredients

For Dressing

2 tablespoons Extra Virgin Olive Oil
2 tablespoons Fresh Lime juice
1 tablespoon Organic Honey
Sea Salt, to taste
Freshly Ground Black Pepper, to taste

For Salad

2 Apples, spiralized
4 cups Fresh Greens
½ cup Fresh Strawberries, hulled and sliced
½ cup Almonds, chopped

Directions

1. In a small bowl, mix together all of the dressing ingredients. Mix together all of the salad ingredients in a separate bowl before mixing the dressing with the salad.
2. Top with the almonds and serve.

Roasted Beets & Tomatoes

This recipe makes delightful wintery spiralized beet pasta for the whole family. This dish is healthy as well as tasty.

MAKES: 2 servings
PREPARATION TIME: 10 minutes
COOKING TIME: 20 minutes

Ingredients

10-12 Cherry Tomatoes
2 tablespoon Extra Virgin Olive Oil
Sea Salt, to taste
Freshly Ground Black Pepper, to taste
2 large Beets, peeled and spiralized
2 tablespoons minced Cilantro Leaves

Directions

1. Preheat the oven to 400 degrees F and arrange the tomatoes on a large baking sheet. Drizzle with 1 tablespoon of oil and sprinkle with black pepper and salt before roasting for 10 minutes.
2. Remove the baking sheet from oven. Arrange the spiralized beets in the baking dish and drizzle with the remaining oil. Sprinkle with salt and black pepper and roast for 8 to 10 minutes.
3. Top with cilantro and serve.

Mixed Vegetable Salad

This dish is an exotic salad with the combination of spiralized vegetables with fresh cherries and strawberries. The use of pecans in this recipe adds a lovely nutty taste.

MAKES: 4 servings
PREPARATION TIME: 20 minutes

Ingredients

For Salad
1 Summer Squash, spiralized
1 medium Zucchini, spiralized
1 Cucumber, spiralized
2 Celery Sticks, chopped
1 small Red Onion, chopped
½ cup Fresh Cherries, pitted
½ cup Fresh Strawberries, hulled and chopped
2 cups Fresh Baby Spinach

For Dressing
2 tablespoons Extra Virgin Olive Oil
1 tablespoon Fresh Lime juice
Sea Salt, to taste
Freshly Ground Black Pepper, to taste
2 tablespoons Pecans, toasted and chopped

Directions

1. In a large serving bowl, mix together all of the salad ingredients.
2. In another bowl, mix together all of the dressing ingredients, except for the pecans. Pour the dressing

over the salad and gently toss to coat.
3. Garnish with the pecans and serve.

Zucchini Coco Chicken Soup

This soup, a warm and comforting dish for the whole family, is packed with the flavors of chicken and zucchini.

MAKES: 2 servings
PREPARATION TIME: 20 minutes
COOKING TIME: 17 minutes

Ingredients

1 tablespoon Extra Virgin Olive Oil
1 Yellow Onion, chopped
2 cups Red Bell Pepper, seeded and sliced thinly
1 teaspoon Dried Thyme, crushed
1 teaspoon Dried Oregano, crushed
½ teaspoon Cayenne Pepper
2 cups Fresh Tomatoes, finely chopped
3 cups Homemade Chicken Broth
2½ cups Organic Coconut Milk
1 cup Homemade Pumpkin Puree
2 cups Cooked Chicken, shredded
2 medium Zucchinis, spiralized
4 cups Fresh Kale, trimmed and chopped
Sea Salt, to taste
Freshly Ground Black Pepper, to taste
3 tablespoons minced Basil Leaves

Directions

1. In a large soup pan, heat the oil on a medium heat. Sauté the onion and bell pepper for 4 to 5 minutes. Add the herbs and cayenne pepper and sauté for 1 minute more. Add the tomatoes and cook for 3 to 4 minutes.

177

2. Add the broth and bring to the boil. Reduce the heat, stir in coconut milk and pumpkin puree, and simmer for 1 to 2 minutes. Stir in the chicken, zucchini and kale and cook for a further 5 minutes.
3. Season with black pepper and salt and garnish with basil before serving hot.

Hot Roasted Jicama

This is a healthier version of jicama, and it is made in such a delicious way! This recipe makes a super healthy and satisfying dish.

MAKES: 4 servings
PREPARATION TIME: 10 minutes
COOKING TIME: 30 minutes

Ingredients

1 large Jicama, peeled and spiralized
2 tablespoons Extra Virgin Olive Oil
1 teaspoon Chili Powder
½ teaspoon Cayenne Pepper
Sea Salt, to taste
Freshly Ground Black Pepper, to taste

Directions

1. Preheat the oven to 400 degrees F and grease a baking dish.
2. Arrange the spiralized jicama in the prepared baking dish. Drizzle with oil and sprinkle with the seasoning. Roast the dish for 30 minutes, turning the jicama after 15 minutes.

Zucchini Roasted Vegetables

*This light and healthy dish makes a nice combination of summery
zucchini and fall sweet potato with asparagus.*

MAKES: 4 servings
PREPARATION TIME: 20 minutes
COOKING TIME: 35 minutes

Ingredients

For Vegetables
*2 Sweet Potatoes, peeled and cubed
1 Bunch Asparagus, trimmed and cut into bite size pieces
1 tablespoon Extra Virgin Olive Oil
Sea Salt, to taste
Freshly Ground Black Pepper, to taste*

For Zucchini
*3 medium Zucchinis, spiralized
1 Garlic Clove, minced
½ cup Fresh Basil, chopped
2 tablespoons Extra Virgin Olive Oil
2 tablespoons Fresh Lemon juice
Sea Salt, to taste
Freshly Ground Black Pepper, to taste*

Directions

1. Preheat the oven to 350 degrees Fahrenheit. Arrange the
   sweet potato and asparagus on the prepared baking
   sheet and drizzle with the oil. Sprinkle the sweet potato
   with salt and black pepper before roasting for 30 to 35
   minutes.

2. Meanwhile, place the spiralized zucchini in a large serving bowl. In a food processor, add the remaining ingredients and pulse until smooth before pouring the basil mixture over the zucchini. Gently toss to coat.
3. Top with the roasted sweet potato and asparagus before serving.

Sweet Potato Bun Sandwich

These bun sandwiches are unique and fulfilling. These are really delicious and even your kids may love them.

MAKES: 2 servings
PREPARATION TIME: 20 minutes (plus time to refrigerate)
COOKING TIME: 30 minutes

Ingredients

3 tablespoons Extra Virgin Olive Oil
1 Garlic Clove, minced
2 medium Sweet Potatoes, peeled and spiralized
Sea Salt, to taste
Freshly Ground Black Pepper, to taste
2 Organic Eggs, beaten
1 medium Onion, sliced into rings
1 medium Avocado, peeled, pitted and sliced
3 tablespoons Almond Butter
4 Tomato Slices
8 Fresh Baby Spinach Leaves

Directions

1. In a large skillet, heat 1 tablespoon of the oil on a medium heat. Sauté the garlic for 1 minute. Add the spiralized sweet potato and sprinkle with salt and black pepper. Cook for 6 to 8 minutes. Transfer the sweet potato mixture into a bowl. Add the beaten eggs and mix well. Transfer the mixture into 4 ramekins, filling half full and covering with wax paper. Place a weight over the noodles to press them down firmly and refrigerate for at least 20 minutes.

2. Meanwhile, in a skillet heat ¼ tablespoon of oil on a medium heat. Add the onion, sprinkle with black pepper and salt and cook for 4 to 5 minutes. Transfer the onion onto a plate and set aside. To the same skillet add the tomato slices and sear for about 2 minutes, turning once after 1 minute. Transfer the tomato onto a plate and set aside. Mix together the avocado and almond butter in a bowl.
3. In a large skillet, heat the remaining oil on a medium-low heat. Carefully transfer the sweet potato bun into the skillet and cook for 3 to 4 minutes. Turn them over and cook for 2 to 3 minutes more. On a serving plate place 1 bun. Spread the avocado mixture over the bun. Place spinach leaves on the avocado and top with the onion rings and tomato slices. Finally place a bun on top. Repeat with the remaining buns.
4. Secure the buns toothpicks before serving.

Coodle Zoodle Patties

These patties are simple to prepare but rich in taste. Zucchini and carrots combine nicely in this dish.

MAKES: 4 servings
PREPARATION TIME: 15 minutes
COOKING TIME: 6 minutes

Ingredients

1 medium Zucchini, spiralized
1 medium Carrot, peeled and spiralized
4-5 Scallions, chopped
2 small Organic Eggs, beaten
½ cup Almond Flour
1 teaspoon Ground Turmeric
Sea Salt, to taste
Freshly Ground Black Pepper, to taste
2 tablespoons Extra Virgin Olive Oil

Directions

1. In a large bowl, except for the oil, mix together all of the ingredients.
2. In a large skillet, heat ½ tablespoon of oil on a medium-high heat before placing ¼ of the mixture into the oil. Press down the mixture to form a patty. Cook for about 5 to 6 minutes, turning once after 3 minutes. Repeat with the remaining oil and vegetable mixture.

Sweet Potato Muffins

This is a wonderfully delicious recipe for grain-free and gluten-free vegetable muffins. These muffins are simple to prepare and nicely combines sweet potato, spinach and egg whites.

MAKES: 2 servings
PREPARATION TIME: 15 minutes
COOKING TIME: 33 minutes

Ingredients

1 ½ tablespoons Extra Virgin Olive Oil
1 Garlic Clove, minced
1 large Sweet Potato, peeled and spiralized
Sea Salt, to taste
Freshly Ground Black Pepper, to taste
3 cups Fresh Spinach, torn
12 Organic Egg Whites

Directions

1. Preheat the oven to 375 degrees F and grease a 6 cup muffin tin.
2. In a large skillet, heat the oil on medium heat. Sauté the garlic for 1 minute. Add the spiralized sweet potato and sprinkle with salt and black pepper. Cook for 6 to 8 minutes. Transfer the sweet potato onto a plate and set aside. In the same skillet, add the spinach and cook for 3 to 4 minutes.
3. Add the egg whites into the prepared muffin cups, ½-inch full. Add the spiralized sweet potato into the cups. Place the spinach over the sweet potato and top with the remaining egg whites. Bake for about 20 minutes.

Sweet Potato Chicken Best

This is one of the best and most versatile dishes for dinner. The spiralized sweet potato makes a nice combination with the other ingredients in this dish.

MAKES: 4 servings
PREPARATION TIME: 15 minutes
COOKING TIME: 16 minutes

Ingredients

1 tablespoon Extra Virgin Olive Oil
½ teaspoon Fresh Ginger, minced
1 teaspoon Garlic, minced
½ teaspoon Cayenne Pepper
1 large Red Bell Pepper, seeded and sliced thinly
1 large Green Bell Pepper, seeded and sliced thinly
1 cup Cauliflower, cut into small florets
½ cup Homemade Vegetable Broth
1¾ cups Organic Coconut Milk
3 Sweet Potatoes, peeled and spiralized
Sea Salt, to taste
Freshly Ground Black Pepper, to taste
2 tablespoons Fresh Parsley, chopped

Directions

1. In a large pan, heat the oil on a medium heat. Sauté the ginger and garlic for about 30 seconds. Add the cayenne pepper and sauté for 30 seconds more. Add the vegetables and cook for 1 to 2 minutes.
2. Add the broth and bring to the boil before reducing the heat and simmering for 4 to 5 minutes. Stir in the

186

coconut milk and sweet potato and simmer for a further 6 to 8 minutes.

3. Garnish with parsley and serve.

Zucchini & Eggplant Chicken

This is an aromatic, warm and tasty dish. The eggplant in this recipe is perfectly roasted and then beautifully combined with the spiralized zucchini and other ingredients.

MAKES: 2 servings
PREPARATION TIME: 15 minutes
COOKING TIME: 25 minutes

Ingredients

1½ cups Eggplant, diced into ¾-inch pieces
2 tablespoons Extra Virgin Olive Oil
Sea Salt, to taste
Freshly Ground Black Pepper, to taste
3 small Garlic Cloves, minced
½ pound Grass-Fed skinless, boneless cubed Chicken
1½ cups Fresh Tomatoes, finely chopped
2 medium Zucchinis, spiralized
2 tablespoons Fresh Basil, chopped

Directions

1. Preheat the oven to 475 degrees F and line a baking sheet with parchment paper. Arrange the eggplant pieces on the prepared baking sheet in a single row. Drizzle with 1 tablespoon of oil and sprinkle with salt and black pepper. Roast for about 25 minutes, turning occasionally.
2. Meanwhile, in a large skillet heat the remaining oil on a medium heat. Sauté the garlic for about 1 minute. Add the chicken and cook for 8 to 10 minutes. Add the tomatoes and cook for a further 8 to 10 minutes. Stir in the zucchini, basil and seasoning and cook for 3 to 4

minutes more.
3. Stir in the roasted eggplant and serve hot.

Squash Tomato Balls

Tomato balls pair nicely with summer squash and cucumber sauce. The fresh mint used in this recipe adds a wonderfully refreshing touch to these tomato balls.

MAKES: 2 servings
PREPARATION TIME: 15 minutes
COOKING TIME: 25 minutes

Ingredients

For Sauce
1 small Cucumber, peeled, seeded and chopped
1 Garlic Clove, minced
1 tablespoon Fresh Basil, chopped
¼ cup Organic Coconut Milk
½ tablespoon Extra Virgin Olive Oil
1 tablespoon Fresh Lemon juice
Sea Salt, to taste
Freshly Ground Black Pepper, to taste

For Tomato Balls
1 cup Fresh Tomatoes, chopped
1 tablespoon minced Mint Leaves
¼ cup Scallion, chopped
Pinch of Dried Thyme, crushed
1 small Organic Egg, beaten
¼ cup Almond Flour
Sea Salt, to taste
Freshly Ground Black Pepper, to taste
1 large Summer Squash, spiralized

Directions

1. Preheat the oven to 400 degrees F and grease a baking sheet.
2. For the sauce, in a food processor add all of the ingredients and pulse until smooth. Cover and refrigerate to chill before serving.
3. For the tomato balls, in a large bowl mix together all of the ingredients, except for the squash. Make your desired size balls from the mixture. Arrange balls in the prepared baking dish in a single row and bake for about 10 minutes. Turn them over and bake for 10 to 15 minutes more.
4. Place the spiralized squash on a serving plate. Pour the chilled sauce over the squash and gently toss to coat. Top with the tomato balls and serve.

Sweet Potato & Pear Pie

This is a unique, delicious and sugar free dessert with the flavors of sweet potato and pears. The spices also add a wonderful flavor to this pie.

MAKES: 2 servings
PREPARATION TIME: 15 minutes
COOKING TIME: 48 minutes

Ingredients

2 tablespoons Coconut Oil, Extra Virgin
1 large Sweet Potato, peeled and spiralized
2 medium Pears, peeled, cored and chopped
4 Organic Eggs
⅔ cup Organic Coconut Milk
1 teaspoon Ground Ginger
1 teaspoon Ground Nutmeg
3 teaspoons Ground Cinnamon
½ cup Fresh Cranberries
1 tablespoon Organic Honey

Directions

1. Preheat the oven to 350 degrees F and lightly grease a 9-inch pie pan before setting aside.
2. In a large skillet, heat the oil on a medium heat and add the spiralized sweet potato. Cook for 2 to 3 minutes before adding the pears and cooking for a further 4 to 5 minutes. Remove the skillet from the heat and set aside. Beat together the eggs, coconut milk and spices in a large bowl. Stir in the pear mixture and cranberries. Transfer the mixture into the prepared pie pan and bake for 35 to

40 minutes.
3. Serve with a drizzling of melted honey.

Roasted Brussels Chicken

This is a trendy and tasty dish of sweet potatoes with chicken and Brussels sprouts. This dish is a perfect balance of chicken with vegetables.

MAKES: 2 servings
PREPARATION TIME: 15 minutes
COOKING TIME: 30 minutes

Ingredients

1 cup Brussels sprouts, halved
Sea Salt, to taste
2 tablespoons Extra Virgin Olive Oil
2 medium Sweet Potatoes, peeled and spiralized
1 Garlic Clove, minced
½ pound Grass-Fes skinless, boneless cubed Chicken
2 cups Fresh Spinach, torn
1 cup Homemade Chicken Broth
Freshly Ground Black Pepper, to taste

Directions

1. Preheat the oven to 375 degrees F and lightly grease a baking dish. Arrange the Brussels sprouts on the prepared baking dish and sprinkle with salt. Roast the sprouts for about 25 minutes.
2. Meanwhile, in a large skillet heat 1 tablespoon of oil on a medium heat. Add the spiralized sweet potato and cook for 8 to 10 minutes. Transfer the sweet potato into a bowl and set aside.
3. In the same skillet, heat the remaining oil on a medium heat. Sauté the garlic for about 1 minute. Add the

chicken and cook for about 10 minutes. Add the spinach and cook for a further minute. Add the broth and bring to the boil on a high heat. Reduce the heat and simmer for 4 to 5 minutes. Stir in the Brussels sprouts and sweet potatoes and cook for a further 2 to 3 minutes. Season with salt and black pepper and serve.

Sweet Potato Apple Bake

This is a fantastic and delicious dessert ideal for special occasions.
Your kids may want this pleasing dessert time and time again.

MAKES: 2 servings
PREPARATION TIME: 15 minutes
COOKING TIME: 40 minutes

Ingredients

2 cups Almond Flour, blanched
1 teaspoon Baking Soda
¼ teaspoon Sea Salt
2 Organic Eggs
¼ cup Organic Honey
⅓ cup Fresh Orange juice
2 cups Sweet Potato, spiralized and cut into 2-inch pieces
1 cup Apple, peeled and grated

Directions

1. Preheat the oven to 325 degrees F and grease a 8x8-inch baking pan.
2. In a large bowl, mix together the baking soda, flour and salt. In another bowl, mix together the eggs, honey and orange juice. Mix the egg mixture into the flour mixture. Fold in the sweet potato and apple.
3. Transfer the mixture into the prepared baking pan and bake for about 40 minutes.

(19)

SPIRALIZE FOR LIFE!

Undoubtedly, the overall health benefits of using the spiralizer to create healthy and creative gluten-free meals are endless. Moreover, preparing meals from spiralized vegetables is a welcome inspiration to the gluten-free and Paleo diets. With this cookbook, you'll be equipped with a variety of meals that are prepared using commonly spiralized vegetables.

Before my discovery of the spiralizer, I was struggling to maintain an interesting and healthy gluten-free lifestyle. For health preservation reasons, I had to avoid gluten, grains, heavy carbs and refined sugars from my diet. Interestingly, my health actually started to improve as I continued on a gluten-free diet, however, my most significant health improvements occurred after I started to incorporate spiralized vegetables in my daily gluten-free eating routine. Consequently, by combining spiralized vegetables with gluten-free foods, I have truly experienced remarkable health benefits. If these recipes have enhanced my health, I firmly believe that it is quite likely that they will also improve yours. As I tell everyone, the spiralizer will be my best kitchen gadget for life! If it ever gets broken, I will happily get a replacement. The rewards of eating vegetable noodles are far more precious than any regular pasta dish temptation.

Thanks again for choosing my cookbook. If you find it to be useful, I would appreciate if you would let other readers know about it. I invite you to join me and countless others on an exciting journey to better health—let's spiralize for a better life!

Happy Spiralizing,
Laura Moore

Made in the USA
San Bernardino, CA
01 March 2015